PROHIBITION IN SOUTHWESTERN MICHIGAN

NORMA LEWIS & CHRISTINE NYHOLM

THE History PRESS

Published by The History Press
Charleston, SC
www.historypress.com

First published 2020

Manufactured in the United States

ISBN 9781467144803

Library of Congress Control Number: 2020941947

For all of the nostalgia buffs who read my books. You're the best!
N.L.

In memory of my beloved parents, Norman and Lydia Bude,
who were young children at the end of the Prohibition era.
C.N.

CONTENTS

ACKNOWLEDGEMENTS

We thank everyone who contributed images and shared information for use in this book. We are so grateful to the public libraries in Battle Creek, Kalamazoo and Muskegon and to Wayne State University, the Kalamazoo Valley Museum, Grand Rapids Brewing Brewery and the Michigan Apple Committee. We also found a treasure-trove of leads in the vertical files. We would also like to thank Andrea Melvin at the Grand Rapids Public Museum.

We also utilized the Kalamazoo, Battle Creek and Muskegon Public Libraries, along with the Wayne State University Library. We remain grateful for the resources provided from the digital collections of the Library of Congress and Wikimedia Commons.

We are grateful for author Chriss Lyons, who wrote the book *A Killing in Al Capone's Playground*, for her help and generosity in sharing some photographs.

We want to send a big thank-you to Paul Drueke for sharing an interesting part of his family's far-reaching history.

We are deeply indebted to our Arcadia and The History Press editor, John Rodrigue, for his endless patience as we put this book together—sometimes under trying circumstances. Without his gentle nudges we'd still be at the drawing board. Also to our copyeditor, Ashley Hill, and cover designer Anna Burrous, and everyone else behind the scenes who work so hard to not only make these books happen but to make them the best that they can be.

Always last but never least, we are indebted to our families and friends for their ongoing encouragement.

INTRODUCTION

Prohibition didn't work in the Garden of Eden. Adam ate the apple.
—Vincente Fox

Beverages containing alcohol have tempted us forever. It is believed that in the first century CE, an alchemist in ancient Alexandria named Mary the Jewess stumbled on the first distillation process. Since her goal had been to turn base metal into gold, she was probably not pleased. Wine is spoken of in the Bible. Shakespeare wrote, "Wine maketh glad the heart of man," to which some wag added, "and it maketh women giggle."

Americans have always objected strenuously to the government meddling in the consumption, production and marketing of alcohol. In 1791, Pennsylvania farmers fought new taxation by tarring and feathering revenue agents in what became known as the Whiskey Rebellion. Closer to home, in Southwest Michigan, long before prohibition became law, various attempts were made to stem the flow—or at least slow it. Those involved were convinced they could ease the suffering of the families, in particular, and society as a whole caused by those who overindulged. Spurred on by organizations like the Woman's Christian Temperance Union, the Anti-Saloon League and the Red Ribbon Movement, some areas voted to make themselves "dry" starting in the mid-1800s. They were unsuccessful, mainly because those charged with enforcement were too often opposed to the idea in the first place. Compromises were

The closed canteen and the open dive called attention to problems that came from closing canteens. *Photograph by artist Udo J. Keppler, courtesy of the Library of Congress 3b49095u.*

made, so some towns in the covered areas were "damp" and others were "moist." Sorting it all out became too cumbersome, and local laws were either repealed or simply ignored.

Events leading up to the Volstead Act included the actions of those in favor of it and those against it—often making for strange bedfellows. Prohibition efforts were supported by churches, the organizations mentioned above, organized crime rings and the Ku Klux Klan. Obviously, the gangsters supported prohibition, as they recognized the once-in-a-lifetime opportunity for unimagined wealth that lay in quenching America's collective thirst. The Klan's support was a public relations ploy to promote an image of law-abiding citizens espousing family values and decency.

On the other side of the issue stood the hardcore drinkers as well as those who simply enjoyed occasionally lifting a friendly glass at their favorite neighborhood watering hole, sipping a bit of bubbly at social events or indulging moderately in the privacy of their own homes. The heavyweights on the opposing side included commercial distillers and winemakers. The largest in number were the brewers, which included forty-seven in Grand Rapids alone. Kalamazoo came in a close second with forty-one. Those in the hospitality industry also knew the Eighteenth Amendment would put them out of business at worst. Even if they switched to a different product line, it would certainly diminish their profits. It's no secret that beer is more profitable than ginger ale.

Within these pages, readers will find some notorious bad guys and some local residents who didn't support the law and believed it infringed on individuals' freedoms. Their shenanigans ranged from producing bathtub gin and operating speakeasies to finding other convoluted ways to, if not break the law, at least bend it to suit their purpose. Their stories will be told against the backdrop of the glamourous (at least in retrospect) Roaring Twenties. World War I was over, and along with the rest of the country, West Michigan was ready for some serious party time. Then, along came spoilsport Andrew Volstead, the congressman from Minnesota's seventh district who ended it all. Whether or not Prohibition was the reason, Volstead was trounced in his bid for reelection.

By the time the Twenty-First Amendment repealed Prohibition, the Roaring Twenties were but a memory. The 1929 stock market crash that ushered in the Great Depression ultimately dulled the roar to a whimper.

1

EARLY ATTEMPTS AND WHY THEY FAILED

We care not for the land, or the money, or the goods; what we want is the whiskey.
—Potawatomi chief Topenbee to Michigan Indian agent Lewis Cass, 1821

The early fur traders did not do the indigenous tribes any favor when they introduced them to alcohol. It didn't take long for the Natives to become dependent on the substance and demand ever larger quantities. Most traders were happy to oblige, but Madame Magdalaine LaFramboise resisted. Her mother was Odawa (Ottawa), and her father was a French Canadian fur trader. When Magdalaine married another fur trader, Joseph LaFramboise, she proved to be a capable partner, as she had an innate business sense and was fluent in French, English, Ottawa and Ojibway. All those qualities enabled her to take over the trading post following Joseph's death.

Her profound Catholic faith prohibited her from supplying Natives with alcohol, as did her Odawa heritage. Magdalaine had seen firsthand the harm drinking had done to her people. She reluctantly compromised when it became apparent the Natives would boycott her business unless she gave in to their demands. She came up with a new product, a watered-down whiskey that contained herbs and small amounts of tobacco. Though she must have still felt guilty, she was able to successfully operate her post on the Grand River, near what is now the Grand Rapids suburb of Ada, Michigan, until she retired. Then, she sold the business to Rix Robinson, an agent of the American Fur Company, which was owned by the New

York Astor family. This was the same Rix Robinson who, along with Reverend William Montague Ferry, is credited with founding the lakeshore city of Grand Haven.

THE BADDEST MAN IN THE WHOLE DANG TOWN

Adam "Pump" Arnold of Battle Creek, who became a major player from the time of his arrival in 1857 until shortly before his death in 1897, never met a law he couldn't break. He was nicknamed Pump because his first business in the city was the manufacturing of wooden pumps. With his brother Martin as a partner, he became quite successful, though that did not stop Pump from doing a bit of loan sharking on the side. Martin Arnold left Battle Creek in 1860, immediately following an incident in which Pump was accused of throwing acid in the face of one of his loan clients who had defaulted. He was never charged with the crime, as there was no way to prove his guilt.

Two years later, Pump opened another business, a public bathhouse next to the pump factory. Over the next few years, he expanded the pump factory. By 1874, he had sold his other businesses to concentrate on what would occupy him for the rest of his life: hotels and saloons. He mainly focused on saloons—both legal and otherwise. His first hotel, the Clifton House, was located on South Jefferson Street, next to the railroad depot. That location proved to be a gold mine when Pump discovered a way to scam passengers. When the train stopped, thirsty men would flock to the saloon, where Pump would take their money. Then, he would claim he didn't have change and would supposedly run to get it. Long before Pump returned, the conductor called out "all aboard," at which time the departing passengers had to decide whether to board the train or remain in Battle Creek and wait for their change. The scam was so easy that Pump couldn't resist enlarging the scheme to pull in even more money. Soon, he was boarding the train to sell sandwiches and liquid refreshments to the travelers who remained on the train. Once again, the train left the station before Pump could scrounge up the change for the bills he had already collected.

Bootlegging followed, and though it was immensely profitable, the greedy lawbreaker also dabbled in arson, prostitution, theft, fraud and assault before murdering his son, George. Even trivial issues that a more reasonable man would overlook turned into new moneymaking schemes for Pump Arnold.

"Woman's Holy War: Grand Charge of the Enemy's Works" was the nineteenth-century crusade for temperance and prohibition. *Currier and Ives, courtesy of the Library of Congress 10163u.*

One would think a career criminal would be too busy to worry about a few pilfered plums, but Pump wasn't. The property line between the Arnolds and their next-door neighbors, the Hamiltons, was in dispute. Pump claimed the plum trees were his. Already known for his short fuse, Pump became enraged when he caught Paulina Hamilton picking what he considered his fruit. He grabbed her arm and yanked it so hard that it was permanently damaged. She sued and won a settlement of $1,500. The plums were probably worth less than a quarter.

Every facet of the alcohol issue was represented in the dysfunctional Arnold family: Pump sold it; his wife, Maria, joined the local Woman's Christian Temperance Union and publicly fought against it; and their son, George, proudly held the post of the town drunk. Despite his other failings, Pump seemed devoted to his wife. To please her, he attended a WCTU rally and took the pledge. It wasn't difficult because he didn't drink, as he was too canny a businessman to allow alcohol to cloud his judgment. After the meeting, he went back to his saloon, hung the "open" sign and began pouring drinks. He had a happy wife and a thriving business. What more could a man want?

Pump Arnold could hold a grudge better than most. Thus began his quarrel with Mayor William Gage. The mayor was also an ordained Seventh-day Adventist minister who took a dim view of those who broke liquor laws. It was unlawful at that time to sell alcoholic drinks in Battle Creek on Sundays or after 9:00 p.m. the rest of the week. One Sunday evening, the mayor disguised himself and went into Pump's saloon and ordered liquor. As soon as he had the bottle in his hands, he removed the fake beard and shabby topcoat. *Gotcha!* Mayor Gage had caught Pump Arnold red-handed. A feud of Hatfield-and-McCoy proportions was soon underway.

It didn't take long for the mayor to find out that the culprit he had exposed would not rest until he had exacted revenge. That came in many forms, but the most comical occurred when Pump and a friend came upon a discarded statue of a shabbily dressed, disreputable-looking man. Pump gleefully shouted, "That looks just like our mayor!" He rescued the statue and placed it on display, thereby setting Gage up for relentless public ridicule. The statue now stands in the Upper Peninsula city of Manistique.

So, why wasn't this known criminal run out of town? The truth is, he once said that if town officials and the newspaper didn't leave him alone, he would liquidate his business interests and leave. No one wanted that to happen. Battle Creek may not have needed Pump Arnold's shenanigans, but it did need the money he poured into the town's economy. Pump Arnold's lifelong crime spree begs the question: if he had lived until after the Eighteenth Amendment was passed, would he have risen in the career criminal ranks to compare with the likes of the Purple Gang and Al Capone, or would those later professional mobsters have looked on him as a pesky fly and orchestrated a plan to leave his body in the same way that his son George's body was found?

MOMENTUM FOR PROHIBITION GROWS ACROSS SOUTHWEST MICHIGAN

The *Michigan Telegraph,* on April 10, 1846, published the "Pledge of the Kalamazoo Cold Water Army":

A pledge we make, no wine to take;
Nor brandy red, that turns the head;
Nor whiskey hot, that makes the sot
Nor fiery rum, to ruin home;
Nor will we sin, by drinking gin;
Hard cider too, will never do;
Nor sparkling ale, the face to pale;
Nor brewer's beer, the heart to cheer;
To quench our thirst,
We'll always bring
Cold Water from the spring;
So here we pledge, perpetual hate
To ALL that can INTOXICATE.

There was never a shortage of those who wanted to stop the flow of the demon rum, but despite their best efforts, there were just as many who easily found ways to circumvent any obstacle placed in their path. One of the earliest organized groups, the Michigan Temperance Society, was formed in 1833 with nineteen branches. The society believed total abstinence was impossible and worked instead for moderation, which they defined as an occasional beer or glass of wine. It backfired because liquor was cheaper and the well-intentioned movement was accused of elitism, and thus, it was forced to line up with those promoting abstinence.

The National Prohibition Convention was held in 1892 in Indianapolis, Indiana. *Photograph by Barnum and Cumback, courtesy of the Library of Congress.*

In the Kent County township of Cannonsburg, several women sued a tavern owner following the misbehavior of their soused menfolk. The *Grand Rapids Eagle* wrote on September 1, 1863:

> *One night last week, quite a number of the women of Cannonsburg, who had become incensed at one "Nat" Robertson, a grocery-liquor seller of that place because of his selling their fathers, husbands, and sons spirituous liquors—keeping a miserable rum hole—gathered together, regardless of law or "any other man," and squelched the concern. It is said they broke into the institution, carefully spilled the corn juice and other strong liquids it contained, and indiscriminately scattered the stock in trade to winds and into the street. "Nat," not being pleased with this operation, came to the city and made a complaint against the fair ones who had so unceremoniously confiscated his liquids and other damp concerns, and yesterday, Sheriff Bailey went to the insurrectionary burg and arrested a number of individuals who were supposed to be the leaders of the rebellion, who bound themselves to report personally today.*

The reporter promised to post updates as the case unfolded, but no such record was found.

Hotel Byron in Byron Center was a popular gathering spot. *Collection of Christine Nyholm.*

Drunkard's Progress shows the decline of a drunkard from the first glass to the grave. *Image by N. Currier, circa 1846, courtesy of the Library of Congress 32719u.*

A similar incident happened in Cedar Springs, a village north of Grand Rapids, when an angry group of women set out to inflict damage on the town's saloons. Their habitually drunken husbands had driven them to the breaking point, and damaging the businesses of those who made them drunk must have seemed like a good idea at the time.

When a proactive saloon owner in Bluffton (now part of the city of Muskegon) heard of these incidents, he decided to take no chances and appeased the women in his area by asking them to sign one of two permits. If a woman signed the first, it meant his establishment would agree not to serve her husband, father, fiancé or whoever she named. That probably wasn't much of a deterrent, as all the would-be patron had to do was find another saloon to frequent. A woman who signed the second permit gave the man in question permission to drink what he wanted, how much he wanted, where he wanted and when he wanted, and she would not hold the saloon owner responsible for any of his misdeeds. It must have been a bit of a blow to a man's ego to need his wife's written permission to imbibe, and it must have been especially humiliating for those whose wives withheld that permission. But hey, the end justified the means.

For a perfect example of conflicting feelings, one has to look no further than the most famous saloon keeper in Kalamazoo. "Dutch" Arnold Van Loghnen ran a successful saloon while he lectured on the evils of drink at the same time. A do-gooder at heart, Van Loghnen was known for inviting newsboys in for hot soup during Kalamazoo's frigid winters. He served free lunches to his drinking clientele, a common practice in those days, as heavily salted food increased thirst, which, in turn, increased profits. The fact that peanuts and pretzels are now offered as bar munchies proves the idea worked. For himself, Van Loghnen preferred ice cream sodas at the drugstore soda fountain, but that wasn't what made him famous in the 1870s. The most startling thing he did was keep a small menagerie in the saloon's basement. One of Van Loghnen's basement residents was a monkey named Jim that he dressed in a snazzy red-and-gold uniform. Jim earned his keep by scampering up and down the bar with a tin cup into which patrons dropped payment for their drinks. Imagine a first timer stopping in for a drink only to see a monkey in livery collecting bar tabs. He probably would have decided he'd already had enough and beat a quick retreat. The real question is why did a man opposed to drinking own a saloon?

Everything changed in 1851, when the State of Maine passed its first prohibition law. *Grand Rapids Enquirer* editor E. Sargeant shared his opinion that alcoholic drink, "with its degradation, poverty, misery, and crime, was an enemy of the public good." But he also thought that such a law would be difficult to enforce in Michigan and believed that those in favor of temperance should rely on moral persuasion. The obvious flaw in his argument was that someone caught in the grip of an addicting thirst would be an unlikely candidate to be morally persuaded.

Maine repealed the statewide law in 1858 and replaced it with legislature that permitted the moderate use of alcohol. In Michigan, the local option law gained favor. It stated that each municipality could decide its own jurisdiction on controversial subjects, including prohibition. An annual referendum on the issue of liquor licensing for the common good was decided by popular vote. The state also allowed counties or municipalities to vote themselves dry or vote for a compromise law that limited the sale and consumption of alcohol, with the exception of alcohol that was used for medicinal purposes. It did little to stop alcohol consumption, as all one had to do was travel to the nearest "wet" spot.

The compromises were not without humor, as each dry community's local lawmakers had to hammer out their own definition of dry. In between bone dry and wet lay several layers. The most lenient offered moderate drinks of any kind. Then, there were the advocates of beer and wine only—and still in moderation. Moist and damp came last, and they were not that far from bone dry. The fun came in watching the court decide if a damp had overindulged himself into the wet camp. Nevertheless, hard-core drys cheered that as the first step toward total prohibition.

On March 26, 1858, the *Ionia Gazette* reported:

> *The temperance movement in Ionia is progressing finely. The meeting that took place last Saturday evening was attended by a large audience and was eloquently addressed by Messrs. J.B. Welch, J.B. Blanchard, A. Williams, O. Tower, L.B. Brown, and others. There appeared to be an entire unity of feeling and a settled determination of those present to maintain the present attitude of hostility to the business of retailing ardent spirits. A committee was also appointed to circulate the pledge through the village.*

In 1860, a short piece in the *Grand Rapids Daily Eagle* made a case for getting rid of a few shanties near the depot and called into play the law that allowed for the removal of public nuisances. The writer claimed that they sold strychnine whiskey and that "other liquids equally strong and murderous are sold at five cents a pint to a set of men that work hard for their money during the heat of the day and then go, of their own accord, or are lured into these filthy resorts, where they spend their time and their money in drinking, howling, and breaking things, generally." He went on to say that one man had recently been stabbed in one of those holes and expressed surprise that there had not been more violence committed by men under the influence of such stimulants. Perhaps, in most cases, the howling and breaking of things had been violent enough, but it didn't matter because if it was a contest, those men were destined to be outdone. A woman named Carrie Nation would later come on the scene for different reasons, and she became the undisputed champion of howling and destroying property.

In 1878, Grand Rapids proprietors of the Rathbun Hotel, A.R. Antisdel and Charles Cummings, were still maintaining a long-held policy that "no spirituous liquors of any kind be served or kept in stock." This was, after all, a place of high moral character. There were also a number of refined young ladies who boarded there during the winter months, and the management may have felt obligated to protect them. That no-liquor policy only stopped people from drinking within the hotel's respectable walls. Gentlemen could still lift their glasses nearby in one of the unsavory bars located in the equally unsavory area known as Grab Corners. It's unknown how many of those refined young ladies were thirsty enough to accompany the gentlemen.

Battle Creek voted itself "dry" in 1853, due in large part to the overwhelming influence of the large Seventh-day Adventist population. The conservative tenets of the faith opposed drinking alcohol due to its negative effects on health and its consideration as sinful behavior. And, yes, the activism of the WCTU ladies, including Maria Arnold, also contributed to the easy passage of the local law.

An article in the *Kalamazoo Gazette* on January 24, 1937, told how the city did not enforce the first dry law between 1855 and 1875; Kalamazoo refused to accept prohibition, even at the highest levels of authority. Some of Michigan's legal community also refused to enforce the law, including Judge Abner Pratt of Kalamazoo. Efforts were again made to reenact the law in 1877 and 1879, but they were defeated each time. Van Buren County voted 2,599 to 1,320 to abolish liquor in 1890. The "wets" tried again in 1892, 1897, 1903, 1906 and 1910, but they, too, were met with defeat in every referendum. Van Buren County remained "dry" for twenty-eight years prior to the enactment of the state prohibition law.

An unnamed man from White Pigeon wrote in 1873 that the village was joining the tidal wave rolling across Michigan. He claimed that on March 8, the friends of law and order resolved to stop the flow of alcohol. They drew up a contract that was signed by the influential men in town,

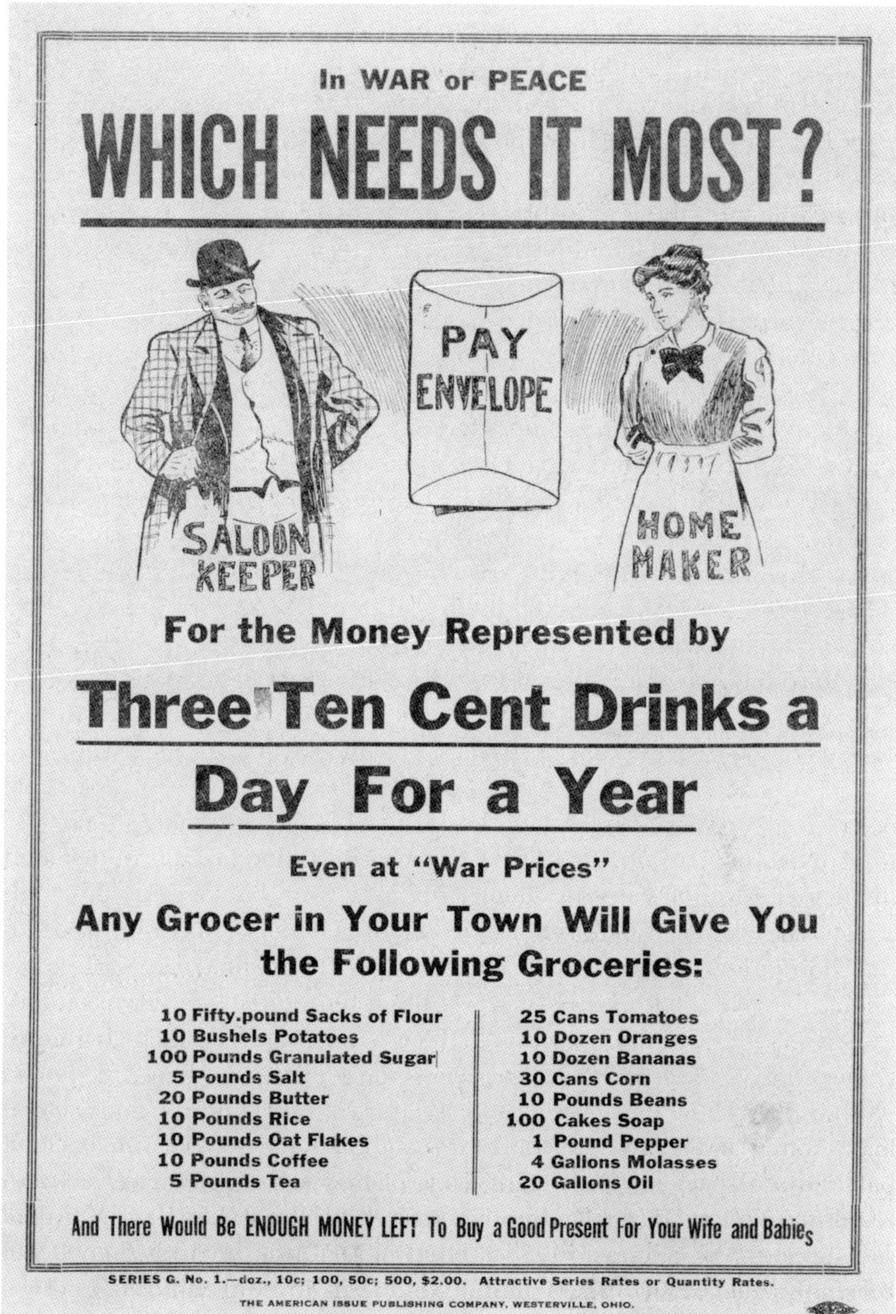

This prohibition poster shows what kinds of groceries could be purchased with the money that was spent on drinks. *Photograph by the American Issue Publishing Company of Westerville, Ohio, circa 1917, courtesy of the Library of Congress 3c18173u.*

This couple holds a sign that reads "Uphold the 18th Amendment." *Photograph by Harris and Ewing, circa 1932, courtesy of the Library of Congress 36699a.*

requesting that local authorities enforce the local law. After the arrest of five men, the writer expressed his opinion that all of the grog shops would soon be permanently closed.

An Allegan resident repeated a rumor he had heard: "There is a report prevailing that someone is soon to make a raid on the liquor dealers, and it is to be hoped our new board of trustees will appoint a good man for marshal this year, one that will perform his duties without fear of the saloonkeepers or any other man or men."

Elsewhere, "Drive the Devil out of Dorr" became the slogan of that Allegan County village. In 1907, the city of Plainwell, which is also located in Allegan County, braced itself for the outcome of the upcoming vote on whether or not to go dry. It had mushroomed into the most contentious campaign in the city's history, and the voter turnout was expected to be close to 100 percent. The drys prevailed by a slim margin. When Sparta went dry, both of the saloons in the city closed. One of the owners saw a need that was not met and vowed to open another outside the city limits.

From Stanton, in Montcalm County, the following report stated:

> *The friends of prohibition have been actively at work for some time. A rather novel temperance move is* [under consideration]. *A temperance man having declared that Professor Mattison's temperance speech should be delivered in every rum hole in the land. Mr. H.W. Luce of Westville promptly offered his hotel and whiskey bar for that purpose, which was accepted by the professor. The whole surrounding community, representing all the various shades of opinion upon the temperance question, are preparing to attend the lecture.*

One major difficulty of enforcing prohibition was that local law enforcement professionals were reluctant to make arrests. Not only was the law unpopular, but in some cases, it meant the officer would dry up his own supply. Dirty cops are not only a present-day phenomenon, as they have been around as long as cops have been around. Some of the non-drinkers in law enforcement were easily tempted by bribes. Like the Volstead Act that followed, the first prohibition laws failed due to law enforcement's unwillingness and inability to enforce them.

East Grand Rapids was home to Ramona Park on Reed's Lake, an amusement park that offered something for everyone, including a merry-go-round, a house of mirrors, ice cream and popcorn stands, a playground and swimming and boating. But the fun wasn't all family-friendly, as the park was also home to risqué entertainment, including dancing and liquor-serving watering holes. Blue laws prohibited the sale of liquor on Sundays. Owners circumvented the law by becoming private clubs, where the local laws did not apply.

This wasn't the park's only brush with notoriety. Members of the Eastern Avenue Christian Reformed Church in Grand Rapids strenuously objected to the Streetcar Railroad Company's plan to operate a dummy line to Ramona Park seven days a week. Not only would the train enable revelers

Interior Department. *Courtesy of the Library of Congress.*

to easily partake in the park's drinking, dancing and gambling, all of which the denomination frowned upon, it would travel so close to the church's property that its Sunday services would be disrupted. When legal means of stopping the plan failed, the church engaged in what became known as the Dummy Line Riot of 1888. When work began, church bells summoned members to the site. As track was being laid at one end, the good church folks tore up track at the other. The church won in the end. As it was later pointed out, the good Dutch people of the congregation were pious and didn't think "remembering the Sabbath and keeping it holy" meant guzzling demon rum on any day—but especially not on Sunday.

Tavern owner Nick Fink of Comstock Park was fined for violations, including serving after legal hours, opening on Sunday and serving minors, but after appearing in court to pay his fines, he went back to work and conducted business as usual.

Emphasizing temperance, not abstinence, the moderate drys frowned on hard liquor but, probably due to the large number of German and other

European immigrants in the city, gave beer drinkers a pass. Brewers took full advantage by advertising their product as a family-friendly beverage and went so far as to call it liquid bread.

In 1907, one of Holland's top pharmacists, Harry R. Doesburg, was charged with selling liquor to minors. When three girls in their teens were arrested for drunk and disorderly conduct, they named Doesburg as their supplier. Around the same time, the city passed new laws that forbade music, shows and entertainment of any kind. It also made it illegal for women to be in a saloon before 8:00 a.m. or after 10:00 p.m. Bowling lanes and billiard parlors were required to be on the first floor of any building saloons occupied, and they were to be separated from any place where liquor was served. Anyone under the age of seventeen was forbidden from bowling or playing pool at those establishments.

State lawmakers folded under the growing impossibility of enforcing prohibition, and in 1875, they repealed the law, preferring a new law that taxed liquor. The legality of local option law was argued in Detroit on July 31, 1875, when Judge Cochrane rendered his opinion that the law should be declared unconstitutional, as it was a tax law, not a license law. He said that the state legislature could tax businesses as well as property, that the tax was a specific tax and that, in his judgment, it was invalid because it was not ordered by the localities. By zealously defying the law, the wets had to see it overturned. That failed to stop prohibition advocates who, on the repeal of the dry law, immediately started a new organization, the Kalamazoo Reform Association, and elected George Buck as president. The local option method of enforcing prohibition had failed, but the idea was by no means forgotten.

2

WHO WANTED PROHIBITION AND WHAT THEY DID TO GET IT

The saloon is a liar. It promises good cheer but sends sorrow.
—Reverend Billy Sunday

Finding Strength in Numbers

Through the years, a number of organizations formed for the express purpose of lobbying for a dry society. The most well-known of these organizations was the Woman's Christian Temperance Union (WCTU), which was founded in Cleveland, Ohio, in 1873. Though "temperance" actually means moderation, the WCTU demanded not moderation but total abstinence. Members were encouraged to wear white ribbons, symbolizing their purity.

The most extreme members of the WCTU were Carrie Amelia Nation and her crazed followers. They entered saloons carrying hatchets and Bibles to carry out what they called hatchetations, or raids on those "rum-soaked, beer-swilled, bedeviled, wicked, riotous, abominations," and they didn't leave until those dens of iniquity had been completely destroyed. At six feet tall, Carrie herself was an imposing figure, and she was made more imposing by her conviction that she was in the right. As she put it, "I felt invincible. My strength was that of a giant. God was certainly standing by me." She then bragged of smashing five saloons with rocks before realizing that a hatchet was the perfect tool for her work. It's no wonder that many saloon owners

A young man is standing between two women, having to choose between purity and the temptation of vice. *Image by N. Currier, circa 1851, courtesy of the Library of Congress 32722u.*

Above: Carrie Nation's feverish zeal for prohibition and her methods of achieving it turned her into a caricature. *Courtesy of the Library of Congress.*

Left: A beautiful poster image of a mother and child is another example of women using children to influence voters on the need for Prohibition. *Courtesy of the Library of Congress.*

posted signs proclaiming: "We welcome all Nations, except Carrie." Yes, there were laws against willful property destruction, and she was jailed numerous times for smashing saloons and for disturbing the peace. She even raised money to pay her fines by selling silver hatchet pins.

Carrie's zeal took root in her daughter's poor health, which she attributed to her first husband's drunkenness. She conveniently overlooked the fact that her own contribution to the girl's gene pool was also less than impeccable. Mental illness raced through her family to the extent that, for a time, her mother believed herself to be Queen Victoria and demanded being treated accordingly. Carrie had her own peculiarities, one of which was her insistence that her work was dictated to her by Jesus. Not in the usual sense that people receive divine callings through prayer; when Carrie spoke with Him, it was always in two-way consultations.

One of Nation's Southwest Michigan appearances took place in Muskegon on August 21, 1902. There, along with her usual diatribe, she condoned the assassination of President McKinley, saying it was a fate befitting the man who supported the brewers. As for his successor, Theodore Roosevelt, she dismissed him as just another "beer-guzzling Dutchman." That was after she wrote scathing editorials about her feelings on the assassination. Not surprisingly, the WCTU and others who had once supported her had long since distanced themselves from the woman they then believed had crossed the line of eccentricity and turned into a raving lunatic. At some point, she changed the spelling of her name and began calling herself Carry A. Nation, and she went so far as to trademark the name, believing that her work would carry the nation away from the evils of drink. Unfortunately, she died on June 9, 1911, at the age of sixty-five, in a mental hospital in Leavenworth, Kentucky, following about four months of treatment. She had worked feverishly for prohibition but didn't live to see it happen.

Most West Michigan women, whether they were WCTU members or not, preferred nonviolent methods of achieving temperance. Some of the ladies made their feelings known by simply swearing that "lips that touch liquor will never touch mine." Others demonstrated, carrying signs bearing that slogan. While Carrie gleefully swung her hatchet, some ladies in Allegan County turned to the legal system instead and tried suing bartenders for enabling their menfolk to become inebriated. They didn't shy away from using the best weapon available to them, their children, in the fight against the demon run. Who could argue that a drunken father was a serious threat to the well-being of his family?

Prohibition advocates found that using children in their campaigns boosted the emotional factor needed to achieve their desired outcome. *Courtesy of the Grand Rapids Public Library.*

Dr. Anna Ballard, a Lansing physician, was already a WCTU member when, in 1887, she was appointed the state superintendent of social morality. The capital city was in obvious need of liquor laws, as Dr. Ballard immediately faced two pressing issues; one was a prohibition law. In the event the law wasn't enacted, the next item on her agenda was to change the drinking age from ten to sixteen. The large number of children who imbibed could probably be blamed on the European immigrants who had fled countries with unsafe drinking water, though, in reality, there were areas in Michigan where the water was also unfit to drink.

One interesting thing about the WCTU was that many of its members were also suffragists. Anna Howard Shaw, who, for a time, lived in Big Rapids, is remembered as being a teacher, the first woman to be ordained a Methodist minister, a medical doctor and a suffragist. With her trademark humor, she put one man in his place when he voiced his concern that women, vain creatures that they are, might sell their votes for a new bonnet. Anna agreed that it could happen. "Who knows? A new bonnet is a fine thing, and any woman would hanker after it." Then, she reminded him that a bonnet cost a lot more than a glass of whiskey, and she had been told

Left: Anna Howard Shaw was a major player in both the temperance and the suffrage movements. *Courtesy of the Library of Congress.*

Right: Dr. John Kellogg and his wife, Ella, operated the famous Battle Creek Sanitarium to advance healthy habits, including, diet, fresh air, exercise and sobriety. *Courtesy of the Battle Creek Public Library.*

that was the current market price of a man's vote. It's no coincidence that the Nineteenth Amendment, which gave women the right to vote, followed closely on the heels of the Eighteenth Amendment.

Another heavy hitter from the WCTU was Ella Eaton Kellogg, the wife of Dr. John Kellogg and the sister-in-law of William Keith Kellogg of cornflakes fame. All of the Kelloggs believed in the regimen of healthy food, exercise and fresh air put forth by the Seventh-day Adventists. The denomination began in Battle Creek, and the city was then its headquarters. For Ella and John, they followed the denomination's principles in the operation of their health resort, the famous Battle Creek Sanitarium, known as the San, where luminaries, including Henry Ford, C.W. Post and Warren Harding, checked in periodically for health tune-ups. Mary Todd Lincoln was a guest on at least one occasion. The use of alcohol and tobacco products was, of course, strictly forbidden.

Lydia Newcomb Comings was born in Spring Lake in 1850. She left the area for college, then taught for a time in Illinois and Pennsylvania. Like Ella

Kellogg, Lydia was an ardent proponent of health, exercise and prohibition. She returned to Spring Lake in 1866, just in time to become a leader in the local WCTU. Lydia didn't limit her activities to Ottawa County but gave speeches nationally as well.

Inspired by Lydia and women like her, on June 10, 1911, a group of Grand Haven residents, including Enno Pruim, David Cline and Thomas Finch, honored the area's WCTU members with a water fountain that was erected on the corner of State and Jackson Streets. The fountain had a cup for people and a trough for horses, and "WCTU, 1910" was inscribed on its base. Its purpose was to remind people that they could quench their thirst without patronizing the neighborhood saloons, and if more incentive was needed, the water was free. Today, the fountain sits on the east side of Jackson Street, between Savidge and Exchange Streets. Its cup has been replaced with spigots, and the trough now serves dogs, not horses.

The Red Ribbon movement also attracted abstainers, and its followers pledged to live alcohol free. The Anti-Saloon League was another popular choice and proved to be instrumental in the passage of the Eighteenth Amendment. Pledges were popular, and each organization had its own symbol for easy identification. The Red Ribbon Society obviously chose red ribbons. Early Woman's Christian Temperance Members wore white ribbons, but at their rallies, everyone who took the pledge was given a temperance pin in the shape of a "T."

Reverend Billy Sunday, a flamboyantly theatrical preacher and a former professional baseball player, made rousing speeches for prohibition throughout Michigan and other states. He believed fervently that all the country's problems were caused by the use of alcohol. He delivered his signature "Booze Sermon" in Lansing the day before a critical vote. The drys won by a landslide.

The Prohibition Party was formed in Michigan in 1869, with Detroit resident John Russell serving as one of its founders and its first national chairman. Three years later, Russell became Pennsylvanian James Black's vice-presidential running mate in the 1872 presidential race. They were defeated by Ulysses S. Grant and Henry Wilson.

The year 1887 saw the passage of legislature that gave every county the right to enact its own laws banning liquor. Van Buren County was the first to take advantage in 1890, with the drys winning with nearly twice as many votes. The issue was voted on five more times in attempts to overturn the ban, but the attempts were defeated, and the county remained dry until the Twenty-First Amendment was enacted in 1933.

This building was used by the local Red Ribbon Society, one of the organizations formed to advance the early prohibition attempts. *Courtesy of the Eaton County Historical Society.*

Billy Sunday poses with the Lansing Police Department. *Courtesy of the Cadillac Wexford Public Library.*

When it became obvious that prohibition was going to become a reality, some tried to make it less restrictive and felt a "moist" law instead of an outright "bone dry" one would be preferable. As an editorial in the *Grand Rapids Press* said, "The moist platform was a safe and sane position, whereas going bone dry, though it aims at a greater good, might overturn the whole situation through excess zeal." The moist measure would allow every person

Lithograph of the Prohibition Party in 1884. *Courtesy of the Grand Rapids Public Museum.*

Principles of Prohibition Party, circa 1888. *Courtesy of the Library of Congress.*

to legally purchase thirty-four bottles of beer, eight glasses of whiskey and twenty-five glasses of wine per month. If that is moist, one can only wonder how they defined wet.

Cartoonist Ray Barnes carried the moist scenario to its natural conclusion when he drew one man single-handedly drinking the entire allotment for one month. The first drawing showed him drinking a beer with several empty bottles on the floor and twenty-five left in the crate. "This is the zeal," he's shown saying. The next shows six empty glasses of whiskey and one full. "It takes a lot of zeal," he says. The third and final drawing pictures a bottle of wine, fifteen empty glasses and he is holding a full one in his hand. "Just a little more zeal and I'll be drunk," he is saying. It should be added that he didn't appear at all upset about the idea.

In December 1908, John Van Dunen was arrested for operating a blind pig, or a speakeasy, on the bank of the Grand River near South Market Street. The establishment was discovered after a stabbing in the Vander Puttee Roadhouse; Frank Mooney and Oscar Badder, two men who were questioned about the stabbing, told the Kent County prosecuting attorney its location. Van Dunen, a bartender for Nicholas Drieborg, was charged with selling liquor without a license. The prosecuting attorney said the password was widely known, and he hoped he would soon be able to charge others with violations.

Strange Bedfellows

The prohibition issue occasionally brought organizations together, creating strange bedfellows. Who would have expected the Ku Klux Klan to align itself with those who favored law and order? Membership was at a record high when the organization's members presented themselves as law-abiding citizens who represented family, home, church and country. This was true throughout Michigan and much of the Midwest, though many tried to hide their membership, as they were embarrassed when they realized they'd made a huge mistake.

The KKK of the 1920s was not the Klan of the 1860s or the 1960s. In the 1920s, members refrained from lynching anyone and never terrorized people by burning crosses on the lawns of perceived enemies. It's estimated that from 1923 to 1925, about 20 percent of the men and 10 percent of the women in Newago County were members. More astonishing is that the leaders of small-town society, especially in Newago and Fremont, were found among those numbers. Judges, sheriffs, police chiefs and officers, teachers, principals, school superintendents, doctors, the Fremont mayor, ministers, newspaper owners and prominent business owners were all active Klan members

Joining the Klan seemed no different to the general population than joining the Benevolent Protective Order of Elks or the local country club. Residents of these rural communities were virtually all white, Protestant and had been born in the United States. The Klan presented itself as a mainstream organization that believed in law and order, prohibition, patriotism and the moral fiber of the Protestant Church—everything the local citizens also held dear. Eventually, the Klan's bigotry toward Catholics, Jews and immigrants became known, and its brief surge of popularity abruptly came to a halt.

3

THOSE AGAINST PROHIBITION AND HOW THEY TRIED TO STOP IT

Prohibition makes you want to cry into your beer
but denies you the beer to cry into.
—Don Marquis

Brewers and distillers were opposed to any form of prohibition and went to great lengths to keep their companies afloat by making sure that everyone knew the large numbers of people who would become unemployed if prohibition became law. The idea of temperance, though widely supported during the Civil War, lost its appeal in the following years. European immigrants were accustomed to drinking beer and intended to continue the practice. The French loved their wine. Many of those habitual imbibers came from places where contaminated water made alcohol a safer choice. The English, both recent immigrants and the progeny of the founding fathers, also didn't want to give up their pints of ale. Hadn't those original courageous Brits come here to escape what they considered too much government interference in their lives? The neighborhood tavern was their American pub, a bolt hole of cheer for those times the wife's chatter or the baby's colicky crying became unbearable.

The Michigan Liquor Dealers Protective Association, founded in Detroit on July 29, 1880, worked tirelessly throughout the state in an all-out effort to protect the right to sell liquor. It wasn't enough to stop the inevitable. Drinking had once been limited to the working class and upper classes. Now, the middle class wanted to join the party. Like the British and Irish pubs,

A woman holds a poster to oppose the Eighteenth Amendment. *Courtesy of the Library of Congress.*

Brewery workers pose with beer barrels at Veit and Rathman's Brewing in Grand Rapids, circa 1890. *Courtesy of the Grand Rapids Public Museum.*

the American saloons often served as the heart of communities. They lured clientele by offering not only liquid refreshment but also newspapers, pool tables, public restrooms and, the biggest draw, free lunch. Saloons were the best place to visit neighbors and learn the latest local gossip.

In 1893, six German breweries merged to form the Grand Rapids Brewing Company. The six breweries included Kusterer City Brewery; George Brandt and Company; the Coldbrook Brewery, owned by the Frey brothers; Veit and Rathman; Tusch Brothers; and Goetz Brewing Company. The consolidation helped the German brewery remain competitive with the national breweries like Anheuser-Busch of St. Louis and Miller Brewing Company of Milwaukee. Innovations such as pasteurization and refrigerated rail cars meant that the large companies could ship their beer across the country. The brewery business, which once had been local, was enabling larger breweries to transport beer to other areas and expand across the country. The large commercial breweries had a competitive advantage because they could sell their brews more economically than their smaller competitors. Numerous small breweries closed as the end of the nineteenth century approached.

This house was lived in by the Frey family, who owned the nearby Frey Brewing Company in Grand Rapids. *Courtesy of the Grand Rapids Public Museum.*

Grand Rapids Brewing Company built a magnificent building, designed to look like a Rhineland castle, on the corner of Michigan Street and Ionia Avenue, which is currently the location of the state office building. The abundant supply of refreshing local spring water was key to producing their popular flagship beer, Silver Foam. Grand Rapids Brewing Company was a success story and became one of the biggest breweries in the Midwest. The brewery had an impressive annual capacity of three hundred thousand barrels of beer, and business boomed. The company ceased brewing beer in 1918, with the advent of prohibition in Michigan. It switched to selling soda and industrial alcohols, eventually closing during the Prohibition era. The brewery had 106 employees in 1917, so the advent of prohibition affected the ability of working people to make money and support their families.

Furniture City Brewing Company, also in Grand Rapids, had thirty-two employees in 1917, according to the U.S. Department of Labor. This brewery, which opened in 1905, was closed in 1919, shortly after the beginning of Prohibition. The brewery took its name from the fact that Grand Rapids

The Tusch Brothers Brewery was one of six breweries that merged into the Grand Rapids Brewing Company. *Courtesy of the Grand Rapids Public Museum.*

Brewery workers pose in front of the beer barrels at the National Brewery, circa 1890. *Courtesy of the Grand Rapids Public Museum.*

This colorful picture of a girl with a goat is an advertisement for Bock Beer for the Grand Rapids Brewing Company. *Courtesy of the Grand Rapids Public Museum.*

This colorful trade card shows some of the products produced by the Grand Rapids Brewing Company. *Courtesy of the Grand Rapids Public Museum.*

was known as Furniture City until most of the manufacturers were lured to North Carolina. It is also sometimes called Calder City in honor of the Alexander Calder stabile located downtown in Calder Square. The Calder stabile was not installed until the 1960s. Today, Grand Rapids answers to a new name: Beer City.

Other breweries listed by the U.S. Department of Labor in 1917 included: Anheuser-Busch Brewing Association, with five employees, and Peterson Brewing Company, with twenty-four employees. Muskegon Brewing Company, in nearby Muskegon, employed twenty people.

The Val Blatz Brewing Company in Grand Rapids was a division of the famous Milwaukee-based brewer. The company is listed in a 1928 city directory as a manufacturer of soft drinks, according to information in the collection at the Grand Rapids Public Museum. The brewery was

Christian Schmitt poses behind the bar at Schmitt's Saloon on Burton Street, Southwest, in Wyoming Township, circa 1900. *Courtesy of the Grand Rapids Public Museum.*

Val Blatz Brewing Company in Grand Rapids was part of the famous Blatz Brewing Company in Milwaukee, Wisconsin. *Courtesy of the Grand Rapids Public Museum.*

able to survive the Prohibition era by selling other products. When the manufacturing of alcohol was once again legal, it returned to brewing beer.

Kalamazoo was a city with several local breweries during the 1800s, including Burchnall Brewery, Robert Walker's Plank Road Brewery, Slater's Brewery, George Judge's Kalamazoo Malt House, the Kalamazoo Spring Brewery, Wagenman Brewery, the Kalamazoo Steam Brewery and more. In 1904, the City Union Brewery, formed by Alfred G. Neumaier in 1896, was converted into the Kalamazoo Brewing Company. By the beginning of the twentieth century, this was the only remaining brewery in Kalamazoo.

As the temperance movement grew, the Kalamazoo Brewing Company tried to position its beverage as a healthful "temperance drink," a low-alcohol alternative to hard liquor. The savvy brewery advertised its beverage as healthful and touted its use of pure, clean ingredients. In April 1915, the City of Kalamazoo voted to outlaw the manufacture and sale of alcoholic drinks. This was five years before the national Eighteenth Amendment was enforced. In Kalamazoo County, sixty-five establishments involved in the sale of alcohol closed on May 1, 1915. The closed businesses included thirty-four saloons in the city of Kalamazoo and Kalamazoo Brewery, the only remaining brewery in the county.

City Union Brewery in Kalamazoo. *Courtesy of the Kalamazoo Public Library.*

Above: Men working with beer barrels at Kalamazoo Brewery. *Courtesy of the Kalamazoo Public Library.*

Left: The medallion with horses and a bottle opener from the Kalamazoo Brewing Company advertises "The Brew from Kalamazoo." *Courtesy of the Kalamazoo Public Library*.

Kalamazoo Brewing Company opened its brewery at John and Walnut Streets and experienced rapid growth before being sold to George Neumaier, who relocated the company to a larger facility on Portage Avenue. Neumaier's son, Alfred, took over the brewery in 1896 and advertised, "The Kalamazoo Brewing Company sells thirsty customers the biggest schooners in town." He continued serving those oversized brews until Michigan ratified the Eighteenth Amendment in 1915.

Between the saloons, brewers and distillers stood the wholesalers. The Grand Rapids–based Drueke-Lynch Company, located at 13–15 Southwest Ionia Street in the building known as the Blodgett Block, had an impeccable reputation and was known and respected throughout the country. The "Drueke" in the name was William Peter Drueke, who emigrated from the German Westphalian town of Niederhelden in 1871. In 1883, William Peter Drueke started his own wholesale liquor business with Alexander Kennedy called Drueke & Kennedy, and it was located on the east side of the Grand River at 25 Canal Street, now Monroe Avenue Northwest. The business soon relocated to 76 North Waterloo Street, now Monroe Avenue Northwest, between Fulton and Lewis.

In 1888, William Peter Drueke and Alexander Kennedy dissolved their partnership, and the business moved to 16 and 18 Crescent Avenue. In 1897, the business moved to 30 North Ionia Avenue Northwest, and the name changed to the Wm. Drueke Company. From 1903 to 1909, the company operated in retail as well as wholesale business. In 1911, the name was changed again to Drueke-Lynch Company and moved a block south to 13–15 South Ionia, a building that is now known as the Blodgett Block. The company was known for its private labels that it created for select clientele, including the Lakeside Club Bouquet, which was served at the prestigious Lakeside Club on Reed's Lake in Ramona Park.

After fifteen years in business, Drueke-Lynch was forced to close on April 30, 1918, the last day alcoholic beverages could be purchased legally in Michigan. They held a large going-out-of-business sale, which, according to the poster, included the company's entire stock of wines, liquors and glassware. It suggested that buyers consider the consequences of the prohibition law with this warning: "Alcoholic liquors for medicinal purposes are a necessity in every household. Ask anyone who has had to live in a prohibition what they had to pay for liquors after the state went dry, and they will tell you from ten to fifteen dollars a quart. Protect yourself against these exorbitant prices."

While that was the end of Drueke-Lynch, it was by no means the end of the large Drueke family's far-reaching impact on its adopted city. William Peter's sister, Anna, married Frederick William Wurzburg, whose Wurzburg's Department Store was a downtown staple from 1949 until 1974. Another marriage connected the family with the furniture hardware Knape and Vogt Company. William Peter's son, William Francis Drueke, inherited the entrepreneurial spirit and established Drueke Games, which produced finely crafted chess and cribbage sets, among other board games. Though now owned by the Carrom Company in Ludington, Michigan, it still carries the Drueke name.

4

BOOTLEGGING, BLIND PIGS AND BATHTUB GIN

Prohibition goes beyond the bounds of reason in that it attempts to control a man's appetites by legislation and makes crimes out of things that are not crimes.
—Abraham Lincoln

The Volstead Act stated that "no person shall manufacture, sell, barter, transport, import, export, deliver, furnish, or possess any intoxicating liquor except as authorized by this act." There were few exceptions, and the law had been carefully drafted to cover any and all ways a person could acquire and consume beverages containing alcohol.

Contrary to popular opinion, Andrew Volstead did not draft the Eighteenth Amendment. He sponsored it, but its primary author was Wayne Wheeler, the head of the national Anti-Saloon League. Though a slight man at a height of five feet and six inches, Wheeler was called a locomotive in trousers due to the tenacity with which he fought to turn off America's taps. In the period following World War I, Wheeler liked to say, "Some of the Germans are still our worst enemy. The most treacherous of those are named Schlitz, Blatz, Budweiser, and Pabst." Actually, anti-German sentiment still ran high. Some people boycotted pretzels, as the name of the snack was German. Another name issue occurred with German measles; one doctor proposed renaming the disease victory measles or liberty measles to honor America's victory in World War I.

While people may have been persuaded to go along with those issues, the majority never agreed with banning beer, especially since Germans were

The Honorable Andrew H. Volstead was credited with the Volstead Act. *Photograph from the Harris and Ewing Inc. Collection, courtesy of the Library of Congress.*

considered the best brewers. Along with the ones Wheeler mentioned, the local front included Kusterers, Brandt, Tusch and Goetz, to name but a few. These industry giants may have honed their craft in Germany, but they were then residents of the United States; forgoing their golden brews would have been the equivalent of the clichéd cutting off your nose to spite your face.

On May 1, 1918, Michigan, nearly two years ahead of the rest of the country, ratified prohibition, but not without a lot of bickering about how it should work. In January 1917, the *Grand Rapids Press* ran an article ridiculing the "sprinklers" who campaigned for compromise:

> *The dry "prohibition" bill is now before the legislature. It is about twice as wet as the average Michigander ever was before and is a blow to intemperance. This present 50-50 proposition would license every Michigander, so-minded, to a jag that would never stop short of delirium tremors. This is what those dry, drys mind you, propose to allow each of us to drink: Once a month, we can have one pint of whiskey—enough to kill an ordinary mortal. Or we can have one gallon of wine—enough to set a whole galaxy of wiggly, wobbly stars in any man's befuddled firmament. Or*

This woman with signs was petitioning Congress to modify the Volstead Act, circa 1932. *Photograph from the Harris and Ewing Inc. Collection, courtesy of the Library of Congress.*

> *we can have three gallons of beer—about sixty-eight average glasses—two or more a day for the continuous drinker—or a superb souse for the intensive individual who believes in concentrated effort. And this is prohibition?*

The issue of compromise played out in Muskegon in the disagreement between the Anti-Saloon League and the Muskegon Rescue Mission.

William Van Domelen, the superintendent of the mission who also chaired the Muskegon County "dry" committee, was in favor of absolute prohibition or "bone dry." He opposed the legislation put forth by Anti-Saloon superintendent Grant Hudson, which included compromises. "I am utterly out of sympathy with the stance of the Anti-Saloon League, as the people of Michigan voted 'dry' and will accept nothing less," he said. "They want it bone dry." The part he fought was that Michigan breweries and distilleries would be shuttered while those in other states could still ship their product into Michigan. That, of course, changed when prohibition became national law.

One thing the lawmakers hadn't counted on was the lack of support from the general public. While they probably knew the confirmed alcoholics would find a source (and so, too, would the more casual drinkers who only imbibed socially), it must have come as a shock when citizens who could take it or leave it decided they'd rather take it. Even some nondrinkers believed the law to be unfair. Even more surprising was that those who had never touched the hard stuff now wanted it. Chalk it up to human nature, but there were people who began drinking just because the powers that be told them they couldn't. By denying people the use of alcohol, the law created a craving where none had existed before.

The Lansing press weighed in on the topic by warning that, should the moist compromise become law, it would "be forever lawful to give liquor to any boy, girl, common drunkard, posted person, locomotive engineer, electric motorman, jitney driver, member of the fire department, policeman, in fact, anyone at all." Of course, not everyone agreed that it was a bad idea.

Even before the act was passed, paternalistic owners of large companies felt duty bound to make sure their employees behaved themselves both on and off the job. The rationale was that they would be both happier and healthier and, therefore, be better workers. Some, like carmakers Ransome E. Olds of Lansing and Henry Ford of Detroit, took it to the extreme and hired spies to make sure all employees complied. They made it known that a mere smell of alcohol on a worker's breath, being seen drinking in a saloon or being seen buying a bottle to enjoy at home meant automatic dismissal. Ford went so far as to say that if the country repealed Prohibition, he would close his manufacturing plant so as not to "put automobiles into the hands of soggy drunks." He didn't, of course, but time has proven that he was right about the dangers of soggy drunks driving cars.

The day Michigan went dry, the *Grand Rapids Press* reported that city saloons had closed. One on Division Avenue hung a banner that said,

"Gone, but not forgotten." The *Press* went on to say that throughout the state, more than 3,200 bars were shuttered and 8,400 men who had made or served booze were unemployed. On May 30, the *Press* wrote of an inebriated man who had appeared in police court after getting drunk on bay rum, an alcohol-laced grooming aid.

Other substitutes people were willing to try included alcoholic flavoring extracts, spirits of camphor, solidified alcohol, Jamaican ginger, liquor tonics and rubbing alcohol, all of which are dangerous in large quantities and some of which are unsafe in any quantity. In 1873, an elderly man discovered a bottle of carbolic acid in the Grand Rapids Police Station. The department used the chemical for cleaning and fumigating jail cells. He drank some of his find and would have died had he not received immediate medical care. It was reported, "He was badly demoralized for some time."

Kalamazoo said goodbye to forty-eight saloons, most of which were located on Saloon Row on East Main Street, including John Frank's, a local favorite that claimed to sell liquor by the gallon, a boast that probably explained its popularity.

On January 16, 1920, a notice in the *Grand Rapids Press* noted that prohibition was the law of the land as of midnight. It went on to say, "The first recorded arrests occurred in New York at 12:05 on January 17. Funeral services for 'John Barleycorn' took place on the preceding Sunday. Stocks of alcohol have been seized, and an enforcement squad numbering 1,500 is employed to help to enforce this seemingly unenforceable law." As if to prove that Prohibition was indeed an unenforceable law, less than three months later, the *Grand Rapids Press* ran a story on the arrest of George Cummerow, a special agent in charge of the Grand Rapids Office of the Department of Justice, for serving whiskey to guests in a Pantlind Hotel room. Cummerow had just returned from the Upper Peninsula, where he had investigated the suspected rum rebellion in Iron River. If a person charged with upholding law can break it, what's to stop the average man with an unquenched thirst from thinking he can do the same? On the same night, March 3, 1920, Charles Gillette (also known as the King of Grand Rapids Bootleggers) was also arrested and defiantly threw a liquor bottle in the street as he was taken into custody.

Adding insult to injury, the rum rebellion that had taken Cummerow and other law enforcement officials to Iron River, a mining town in the Upper Peninsula, never happened. It all started a few weeks after the Volstead Act went into effect. Local constabulary officers, the forerunners of the state police, found three barrels of wine in the home and store of the Scalcucci

A masked criminal at the grave of John Barleycorn holds a knife and a gun as he shoots at a fleeing pilgrim. *Photograph by Ralph Barton, circa 1921, courtesy of the Library of Congress 3b52743.*

family in Iron River and confiscated it. Because the police intended to have the family prosecuted, they asked the state's attorney, John McDonough, to hold the evidence. McDonough didn't agree and said the Scalcuccis were allowed to have that much alcohol for personal consumption and that because they hadn't sold it, no law had been broken. The constables promised to come back with armed U.S. agents. For ten days, the story captured the attention of reporters across the country. Newspapers everywhere ran headlines stating, "WHISKEY RIOTS IN MICHIGAN, ARMED FEDERAL AGENTS INVADE MICHIGAN TO ENFORCE DRY LAWS," and, "U.S. AGENTS WILL CRUSH BOOZE REVOLT." Even the *New York Times* reacted with, "RUM REBELLION HAS SUBSIDED," and, "IMPROVISED WHITE FLAGS FLY OVER WET STRONGHOLD IN MICHIGAN."

Iron River, like most of the state's mining areas, was heavily populated with European immigrants, including the Italian Scalcuccis. Feeling the village was under scrutiny by the whole country, anyone who had the slightest amount of alcohol, even perfectly legal whiskey that was set aside or used as a cough suppressant, immediately dumped it. Women got rid of their cooking sherry. So great was their fear of being deported, they hung all manner of white flags to indicate their surrender. When the agents came, the only alcohol left in Iron River was that which belonged to the Scalcuccis, and it was still locked up for use as evidence of a crime that had not been committed.

In the end, Iron River was declared "dryer than the Sahara Desert." The Italian wine was returned to its rightful owners, as it was made before Prohibition and was for their personal use only. The whole thing had only been a power struggle between two men, neither of whom wanted to blink first. Boys will be boys. The historic nonevent is still celebrated annually in July as the area gears up for Rum Rebellion Days. Decades later, Margaret Scalcucci represented her family as the grand marshal of the Rum Runners Parade.

In 1920, *Survey* magazine selected Grand Rapids as a model city to espouse the benefits of Prohibition. The article claimed the city had virtually no unemployment, little default on mortgages and plenty of support of local schools and churches. In retrospect, it wasn't that the good citizens of Grand Rapids obeyed the Prohibition law as much as that few of the lawbreakers had been caught. That was proven when the city's police department's liquor enforcement department saw a sharp decline in drunkenness arrests during the early days of Prohibition. Those arrests rose significantly as a blatant disregard for the law spread.

Most of Michigan's illegal booze came into the state from Canada via the Detroit River and Lake St. Clair. While Canada had its own prohibition laws concerning consumption, the manufacture and exportation of alcoholic beverages was legal. The Purple Gang of Detroit controlled the pipeline, but those in need of smaller quantities of alcohol smuggled Canadian liquor in fake gas tanks, hot water bottles and hollowed-out bricks. One small-time smuggler simply removed a bench in his boat and replaced it with cases of whiskey; then, he covered the cases with blankets and made his kids sit on them. Hiding in plain sight, they looked like a father and his kids enjoying a fishing outing. Construction of the Detroit-Windsor Tunnel began in 1928, and it was completed in 1930. It proved so beneficial to smugglers that it earned the nickname the Detroit-Windsor Funnel.

The United States–Canada connection in illegal booze became more complicated when Ontario passed the Liquor Control Act, severely limiting alcohol consumption. That gave the criminal element another angle to work. In what was called "short circuiting," some criminals profited by smuggling

Men in a brewery setting. *Courtesy of the Library of Congress.*

liquor out of Canada, only to turn around and sneak it back in. Some of the scofflaws had an entrepreneurial bent and realized early on that there was no reason to enter Canada in an empty boat, and they profited by smuggling tobacco, cigarettes and other contraband into the country. In Canada, it was legal to produce and export liquor but not to sell or consume it at home.

Rumrunners who found themselves in immediate danger of being caught switched to "Plan B" and abandoned their cargo—sometimes, just by throwing it overboard. That led to the problem of broken glass in the waterways (and maybe some inebriated fish). If time allowed, the lawbreakers had devised a system of intentionally releasing the goods overboard to be retrieved later. Because cases were harder to retrieve, they came up with a way of tying together strings of bottles. Some packed the bottles in fishing nets. This meant some of the abandoned cargo, along with what was lost in shipwrecks, provided many an impromptu party when the sunken spirit-filled barrels and bottles washed up on shore. Few, if any, reported their finds, which led to a prayer: "Lord, it's a dark and stormy night and we pray all mariners will safely reach their ports, but Lord, should there be a shipwreck, could you see your way to let it happen here."

So much of the liquid product was diluted or had other things added that one bootlegger stood out among the rest. Bill McCoy provided untainted liquor of top quality, and from this came the term "the real McCoy." One concoction that was the opposite of the real McCoy was called the coroner's cocktail, which was made with wood alcohol as the primary ingredient. It was guaranteed to "put a he-man plumb coo-coo, dead drunk or dead and drunk." It didn't help that it was often transported in car radiators.

The article titled "Michigan, Soused and Serene" in the March 1930, 1918 edition of *Plain Talk* says it all. Written by Walter Liggett, who was called the last of the muckrakers, the scathing report attracted the attention of state officials who then tried to keep it out of the state. They did this by threatening the local distributor. Evidently, those Lansing guys were slow learners. Prohibition itself still hadn't taught them that banning something only increased demand. The magazine hired its own drivers to circulate the issue in dispute. It was later reported that fifty thousand copies had been sold in Michigan. "People borrowed issues, resold them, and rented them out for fifty cents a day." One Michigan editor estimated that some three hundred thousand Michiganders had read the article.

Had the rumrunners operating on the Detroit River used their business acumen in a legal enterprise, they could have been as successful as Henry Ford and Ransom E. Olds. One example of their skill was the perfectly timed maneuvers in docking and unloading contraband. Starting with a daring sprint in speedboats from Canadian waters to a United States dock, their well-trained teams consisted of "Airedales" who signaled the "monkeys" when it was safe to land their cargo without getting caught. "Gorillas" then guarded the landing site, where a long line of cars waited to be loaded. After the cars were packed, "gorillas" stopped traffic while the booze parade made its hasty departure. Including the time it took to load the waiting cars, the whole operation took less than four minutes.

Once the Volstead Act was passed, organized crime played a major role in the sale of alcohol. The Purple Gang of Detroit controlled the eastern part of the state as far west as what is now Highway 131, running north and south through cities including Cadillac, Big Rapids, Grand Rapids and Kalamazoo. Chicago's Al Capone had his fingers in the pie from there to Lake Michigan.

One result of the Volstead Act was the dangerous substitutes people used when they couldn't get their first choice of liquid refreshment. Pharmacists in Lansing and Holland were arrested for supplying alcohol to their customers for nonmedicinal purposes. Rubbing alcohol, hair tonics, cologne and heating alcohol were among the choices the most desperate tried and didn't always survive. The act also led to enterprising citizens constructing and operating their own stills. Moonshine from homemade stills had been, until then, associated with entrepreneurs in the Appalachian region and was called moonshine because it was made at night to avoid detection. The stills themselves were simple apparatuses consisting of a metal pot and a condensation coil. Corn mash was boiled in the pot before being routed to the coil, where it was then drained into bottles or other containers. During Prohibition, the process was done in kitchens. Bottles were often too tall to fit under kitchen sink spigots, so the distillers had to use bathtubs to bottle the product, leading to the term "bathtub gin." It was never meant to describe a bathtub as an oversized punch bowl of forbidden drink.

Prohibition was sometimes called the "Noble Experiment" because President Herbert Hoover described it as "a great social and economic experiment, noble in motive and far reaching in purpose." That was a nice sentiment, but it's unknown how he described his own habit of frequently having a cocktail or three at the Belgian Embassy. He didn't break any laws because, technically, embassies are not considered to be on United States soil, but it does raise the question of how strongly he believed in what he called the noble purpose of the act.

PARTYING HEARTY IN THE ROARING TWENTIES

Some viewed the 1920s as a time to party. The Great War was over, and though there were growing indications to the contrary, the general public didn't want to think that such an atrocity could ever happen again. Eat, drink and be merry was the mood, with emphasis on "drink," as everyone knew that making merry was more fun when those participating were well-lubricated. One hundred and twenty prohibition law violations were issued in Kalamazoo. By 1927, with the sheer number of violations of the Prohibition law, state legislators decided more stringent penalties might halt, or at least lessen, the ever-escalating crime wave and passed the Habitual Criminal Act. This meant that former misdemeanors would be tried as felonies. Perpetrators would no longer get off with a fine or a warning.

Speakeasies and blind pigs were everywhere. Initially, blind pigs were frequented by men who paid to see the pig and were then handed a free drink. Speakeasies welcomed everyone they trusted. Over time, the terms came to be used interchangeably. Some were operated like nightclubs,

The concerns of the women of the WCTU's were fueled in part by prostitutes, like this one, in lumber camps. *Photograph from the collection of Christine Nyholm.*

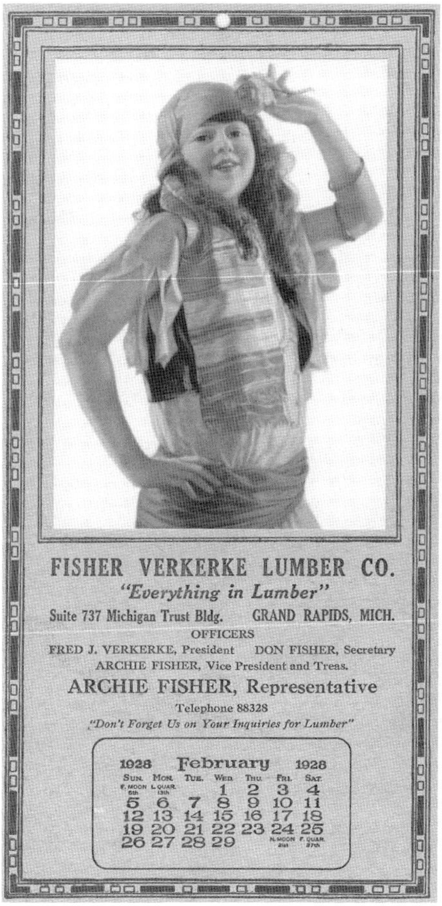

Left: Fashionable women, like this one, flaunted their independence. *Photograph from the collection of Christine Nyholm.*

Right: Fashionable women had short bobbed hairstyles during the 1920s, as seen in this calendar photograph distributed by Fisher Verkerke Lumber Co. in Grand Rapids. *Photograph from the collection of Christine Nyholm.*

with jazz bands and good, clean (except for the hooch) fun. The seedier establishments also dabbled in prostitution. Restaurants often had separate businesses on their second floors or in their basements, and anyone who knew the password could easily gain entry. Some establishments issued membership cards to trusted patrons. It also wasn't unusual for individuals to set up illegal saloons in their houses; some were open every night, others for special party nights. As long as the neighbors were invited they weren't

Left: In a clever play on words, a pair of "bootlegs" was found in the office of Lincoln C. Andrews. Miss Hattie Klawans was a clerk in the office of the prohibition czar, and she wore her new Russian boots. *Courtesy of the Library of Congress 3b43166u.*

Right: A woman hides a flask in her Russian boot. *Photograph from National Photo Company Collection, courtesy of the Library of Congress 3b44030u.*

likely to complain. Card tables were sometimes set up in other rooms so that if the police came knocking, the crowd could be explained as a bunch of friends enjoying a night of poker or bridge.

Prohibition had the unexpected result of fostering freedom from the restraints of Victorian mores, especially among women. These freed women were called flappers, and they introduced a new look in fashion by gleefully abandoning their restrictive undergarments in favor of dresses that were short enough to show kneecaps and hung loosely on bodies that were no longer encased in corsets. These women even bobbed their hair. Initiated in the 1920s, the term "flapper" described women who flamboyantly flouted their contempt for what polite society deemed conventional behavior. Men wore raccoon coats. Everyone carried a flask; men kept them in their pockets, while women brazenly stuck theirs in their garters. It was joked that when tailors measured their clients for new suits, they asked if the gentlemen wanted the pockets to be pint- or quart-sized.

The Roaring Twenties (also called the Jazz Age) weren't all about drinking bathtub gin; behaviors changed as well. Women felt free to smoke in public and wielded stylish cigarette holders as fashion accessories. Dancing was a natural accompaniment to drinking and smoking, and jazz clubs flourished. Couples danced the Charleston and shimmied at dance marathons, often lasting for days. The Lindy Hop was popular then, and in later years, it became known as the Jitterbug. In addition to their choices in fashion and entertainment, flappers wore heavier makeup than their more conservative sisters, and they drove cars. When a gentleman caught a flapper's eye, she elevated the art of flirting to more than dropping a handkerchief or holding her fan a certain way. While some called them brazen, to others, they were a welcome breath of fresh air. This was the same decade that ushered in talking movies and Mickey Mouse; popular songs included "Ain't Misbehaving" and "Making Whoopee"; Ernest Hemingway and Sinclair Lewis wrote best-selling books, along with F. Scott Fitzgerald, whose title character in *The Great Gatsby* acquired most of his immense wealth through smuggling liquor.

5

ENFORCEMENT OF THE VOLSTEAD ACT

We could not enforce the prohibition law in Michigan if we had the whole United States standing army.
—Roy Vandercock, commander of the Michigan State Police, 1930

There were exceptions to prohibition, one being medicinal whiskey. Doctors charged by the prescription, and the vast numbers of prescriptions that were written implied that alcohol was indeed a miracle drug, as so many patients claimed it was the only medicine that provided relief for just about every ailment known to man. Patients were allowed a refill every ten days, and the prescription included strict dosage instructions. One Lansing classic read: "Take 4 ounces every hour for stimulation. Continue to use until stimulated." This wasn't as simple as it sounded, as doctors who wrote too many prescriptions were subject to arrest. All prescriptions issued for alcohol had to be on file in Lansing. Pharmacists were targeted, too, both as robbery victims and as yet another provider of illegal hooch.

Pharmacists were a factor in selling liquor for non-medicinal purposes even before Michigan became one of the first states to ratify the Eighteenth Amendment. In some cases, the doctor simply sold the pharmacist a blank prescription pad, an act that could and did grow exponentially, as forgers created as many pads as needed. In 1909, Holland aldermen Karel and Huizinga announced that drugstores had come under the suspicion of the licensing committee in its fight against the saloons. The committee's members felt that the druggists with complaints filed against

Pharmacies were able to provide liquor legally to customers with prescriptions, which provided opportunities for all kinds of shenanigans. *Courtesy of the Library of Congress.*

them would be unable to hide their unlawful sales from them. They were wrong in underestimating the creativity of men bent on getting what they had been denied through honest effort. The press expressed frustration with the aldermen for not being more forthcoming with information; instead, they answered "no" to every question asked, even though the rumor mill said they were hot on the trail of some of the druggists and would soon force them to stop selling alcohol for any use other than medical. The unidentified source added, "Especially on Sundays, as they believed in keeping the Sabbath holy."

Some thirsty patients discovered the best way to be cured of miscellaneous maladies was to steal a doctor's prescription pad and write their own. Holidays created yet another opportunity for lawbreaking. Various communities decided that celebrating the Fourth of July without booze would be like trying to celebrate the day without a parade and fireworks. *Unthinkable*! Some people believed alcoholic beverages should be offered on all holidays.

Another exception to Prohibition was the use of communion wine, which, of course, set up churches as robbery targets. Communion wine had to be purchased from the government to control its distribution. Church attendance spiked, as those who had never been inside of a house of worship saw this as a simple way to satisfy a desire. Needless to say, they went back to sleeping in on Sunday mornings when they realized they would be served a miniscule amount of wine, not the glass of vino they hoped for. Not all those who bought sacramental wine were legitimate. Pseudo preachers acquired the joy juice but ministered only to themselves or sold it to friends.

HARD CIDER FOR PERSONAL CONSUMPTION

The apple orchards of Michigan offered a plentiful supply of fruit for hard apple cider. European immigrants brought their recipes to the New World and had the knowledge that was needed to turn apples into a beverage that was imbibed in many households. It was normal for children and adults to drink cider in the morning, afternoon and at night. Cider had a low alcohol content that could kill the bacteria that was found in water. Since impure water was the origin of a host of diseases, drinking hard cider was considered safer than drinking plain water.

A man at an orchard learns that the apples are not good for eating but are good for drinking. *Courtesy of the Library of Congress 3b40795u.*

An apple picker at Battle Creek farmer's market probably didn't ask if the intended use was for pies or hard cider. *Courtesy of the Library of Congress.*

Farms in Michigan provided the ingredients for alcohol production. *Courtesy of the Library of Congress.*

Many of the apple trees in the region would have been planted by Johnny Appleseed, who was a real person named John Chapman. The apples used in cider were called spitters because they were bitter and were not considered good eating apples. If one bit into one of these apples, they would likely spit it out in distaste. However, the spitters were the basis for a delicious dry cider, the likes of which is served in Europe to this day. Unfortunately, many of the apple trees were destroyed during Prohibition, partly as a temperance statement and partly to make room on the land for other crops. Sadly, one of the consequences of Prohibition was the loss of this species of apple tree across the country.

Cider has had a resurgence of popularity in Michigan. While the cider mills today produce a good-tasting, refreshing beverage, it is not the same as the European-style beverage that was consumed before the days of Prohibition. Apples are an important crop in Michigan, with orchards producing crops of great-tasting apples. However, they are not the spitters used for the European-style cider that was produced in the early days. The style of cider enjoyed by early settlers is not produced by today's cider mills in America. The old-style cider is still produced in Europe, so you can experience the refreshing beverage if you get a chance to travel to the old country.

Beer: Home Brewing and Breweries

Immigrants from countries such as Germany, Ireland and Italy brought their knowledge of home brewing to America and made their own beer. It was common for immigrants to make their own homebrews from local grains, often storing the homemade beer in their basements. Like hard apple cider, the alcohol in the beer killed bacteria in water, so it was considered healthy to drink the low-alcohol beverage. Many people jovially called beer "liquid bread" because it was made of healthy grains, hops and yeast.

During the mid- to late 1800s, local breweries proliferated in towns throughout Michigan, and they were often operated by German and English immigrants. The brewery business catered to a local clientele because transporting beer over long distances could have damaged the quality of the brew; this was at the end of the Civil War era, and a variety of family-owned operations used horse-drawn carriages to deliver products throughout the region. The trip to Detroit took seven to ten days, and beer barrels were susceptible to exposure to heat, light and motion, which had an adverse effect on the quality of the beer. Therefore, breweries made deliveries in their local areas to ensure quality.

The first commercial brewery in Michigan was founded in Grand Rapids by German immigrant Christoph Kusterer in 1849. The German

C. Kusterer City Brewing in Grand Rapids. *Courtesy of the Grand Rapids Public Museum.*

braumeister was trained in the old-world traditions and brought his skills to the New World. He built the City Brewery on the southwest corner of Michigan Street and Ionia Avenue, a site chosen because of its location above a spring of fresh water that was fed from an aquifer beneath the Grand River. The pure water was key to creating a high-quality beer that was enjoyed by drinkers. Tragically, Christoph Kusterer perished in 1880 while he was traveling on the steamer *Alpena*, which went down in Lake Michigan during a violent storm. City Brewery was carried on by his sons and grandsons.

Christoph Kusterer was the German founder of Kusterer Brewing Company. *Courtesy of the Grand Rapids Public Museum.*

Many breweries stayed in business by switching from beer to ginger ale and near beer, a legal substitute containing less alcohol. Some, including Schlitz, Pabst, Miller, Budweiser, Blatz and Stroh's, added another product to the mix: malt syrup. The syrup was marketed as a grocery product to be used in place of sugar when baking bread and other goodies. Malt syrup is also a beer ingredient, and one can would yield fifty pints. A Lima, Ohio newspaper reported that, in one month alone, enough malt had been sold in that city to make eight hundred thousand loaves of bread. Since that far exceeded average consumption, one could only conclude the approximate population of only forty thousand was drinking far more syrup than it was eating. On July 24, 1928, the Michigan Supreme Court overturned a case in Montcalm County in which a grocer had been convicted of breaking Prohibition law by selling malt syrup. The court decided the syrup was a food product and that, by itself, it was not intoxicating. The court said it only became beer when added to yeast and water. As yeast and water could not be declared illegal, neither could malt syrup. Today, grocers no longer sell the product, but it is available through purveyors of home brewing supplies.

Rock and rye, another homemade drink, was made by adding together whatever whiskey was available, horehound candy, sour cherries, cinnamon, cloves and orange and lemon zest. It would be ready for consumption in about five days, after the candy had dissolved. Its smell and taste made it easy to defend as a needed cough medication. It also did not take long for fruit growers to figure out that they could add water to a crock of fruit and wait for it to ferment. Exceptions to prohibition weren't needed in the beginning. Everyone knew that the law would go into effect in Michigan on May 1, 1917, so all they had to do was lay in a large supply and manage to keep it hidden—or buy alcohol in Indiana or Ohio.

Beleaguered Ramona Park in East Grand Rapids continued drawing the attention of the authorities. It fell under the jurisdiction of the county sheriff to prove what was widely known as an open secret. The fact that alcohol flowed freely in the various clubs was confirmed by neighbors who complained regularly of public drunkenness and disturbing the peace. Kent County sheriff William Smith enacted a midnight curfew; most complied, but the smaller clubs located at Point Paulo did not, and neither did the Rendezvous. Raids proved ineffective, as the owners had inside help from city officials and dirty cops. Eventually, more arrests were made; the Rendezvous owners were forced to permanently close the club; the East Grand Rapids Village constable resigned; and a Grand Rapids police officer was suspended.

Prosecuting attorney Earl W. Munshaw, with help from the Michigan State Police, in the spring of 1926 declared war on what he referred to as Rum Row. With a special agent, he worked undercover surveillance on the Point Paulo area. Rumor had it that the beer taps were still filling the glasses of gamblers. On April 13, Anna Hite and Olive St. Clair were arrested for selling beer at the Griffin Club in the Ramona Park complex. Like others, the company closed at a financial loss to the owners, and its employees suddenly found themselves unemployed.

Governor Fred W. Green, in May 1929, signed into law a bill that gave Michigan the nation's toughest penalties for bootlegging, home brewing or any illegal manufacture of beer or liquor. Violators faced fines of up to $2,000 for a first offense. Repeat offenders were given harsher sentences. It must have seemed like a good idea at the time, but it did little or nothing to halt the illegal making and selling of alcoholic beverages. In fact, it was most likely welcomed as another challenge to keep scofflaws from becoming complacent and therefore careless. Restaurateur Nick Fink in Comstock Park, just north of Grand Rapids, was arrested for several violations, including selling alcohol to minors. He considered the fines nothing more than a cost of doing business.

Fink's tavern has an interesting history. In addition to once being a speakeasy, the building also housed a brothel on the third floor, and it is said to be haunted. Opened in 1888, it is the oldest continuously

Nick Fink's Bar in Comstock Park, founded in 1888, is the oldest bar in Grand Rapids. Al Capone and his men reputedly loved the bar. *Photograph by Christine Nyholm.*

operating restaurant in Kent County, and it was the scene of the county's first recorded flight. In 1905, Nick Fink II built a plane using a bicycle and wings, and he flew off the roof. He stayed aloft long enough for it to count as a legitimate flight, but he crashed when he hit a telegraph pole. The tavern was also one of Ernest Hemingway's favorite watering holes on his frequent trips from Oak Park, Illinois, to Petoskey, Michigan. Not only did he like the moonshine, it's believed some of the characters in his early short stories were based on people with whom he drank illegal booze at the tavern.

Today, with its glory days long gone, Nick Fink's is still a popular local eatery and a favorite spot to enjoy a cold beer after watching a Michigan Whitecaps home game in the nearby Fifth Third Ballpark. The name hasn't changed, though Nick IV was the last family member to own it.

Jackson County's sheriff arrested numerous rumrunners who passed through his jurisdiction while traveling between Detroit and Chicago. He must have been tired of doing all the work while the court got all the money because he decided he could beef up his income by stopping the arrests and charging tolls. It's not a stretch to assume that other officers followed his profitable lead. While charging tolls was pretty much the same thing as accepting bribes, they probably thought it sounded a bit classier. Jackson

Betta Holloway broke the law to ease her police officer husband's pain after being shot by a rumrunner in a routine traffic stop. *Courtesy of Jonelle Rickert.*

County's sheriff wasn't the only cop with a foot on either side of the law. While on duty in Portland, Officer Fred Holloway stopped a suspected rumrunner. The driver shot Holloway in the shoulder. Though the wound was superficial, it hurt badly. Like any good wife, Betta Holloway wanted to ease her husband's discomfort, and she did so by dosing him with a homebrew she procured from a neighbor. And, no, when Holloway returned to duty, he didn't arrest Betta—or the neighbor.

Three men were arrested at the Central Michigan freight yards when they were caught loading railcars with containers labeled "gears." Prohibition agents inspected the containers and found $75,000 worth of wine and champagne. The goods were confiscated, and newspapers had a field day with headlines about the well-oiled gears.

In Grand Rapids, the venerable Peninsular Club was a popular private establishment where the elite male city residents had enjoyed membership for 129 years. Not surprisingly, its members expected to be served alcohol. Even less surprisingly, their thirst was satisfied. Rumor has it that one of the club managers, who shall remain nameless, found out the hard way that the club's prestige didn't protect it from raids. The manager in question took the fall and never ratted out his partners in crime. After serving a short sentence, he learned that his grateful associates had set him up for life. Because most people disagreed with the law anyway, he never suffered the stigma of his ex-con status.

The concept of honor among thieves (and moonshiners) evaporates when a man finds his life in danger. Arch Ramey of Cadillac had a falling out with his partners Cash Holmes and Dell Mitchell, and they threatened to beat him to death. Arch didn't particularly like their plan, so he struck the first blow by telling the local police about their still. The trio produced a pineapple-flavored liquor that the authorities knew about, but they had been unable to identify the makers. The ensuing raid uncovered several gallons of the hooch and two stills along with a loaded rifle. All three men were arrested. Arch said he regretted snitching on his former pals more than he regretted going to jail for bootlegging. The trio had come to Cadillac from the hills of Kentucky, where they had mastered their trade, and snitching was considered a serious violation of the code of the hills.

Arrests were frequently made, but for every blind pig or speakeasy shut down, hundreds remained undetected. Federal judge Fred M. Raymond, in November 1927, ordered four residences to be padlocked in Grand Rapids. Three of them were run by women. All were fined $1,000 and ordered to remain shut down for six months; after that, they could petition to reopen as long as they refrained from running an illegal business.

Lansing police chief Alfred Seymour served from 1917 to 1922 and carried out the standard procedure of pouring seized booze down the drain in headquarters. His men made so many arrests that visitors to the station often complained it smelled like a brewery. Sometimes, the lawmen were even a bit too overzealous in their haste to nail lawbreakers.

In 1924, thirty Lansing state police troopers stormed into Robinson Township in a caravan of five cars and a truck to raid farms. The officers simultaneously broke into both front and back doors so that the alleged desperadoes could not escape. All of the raids took place at 9:00 p.m. to ensure no one could warn the others on the list. Six men were arrested, though at most homes, no liquor was found, and at others, only miniscule amounts were found. At least one farmer was injured. George Van Hall was handcuffed, kicked and hit in the head before being thrown in the truck and taken to jail. The officers confiscated his two-quart can, which turned out to contain only water; he only had a small half-filled bottle of liquor. The victim—or criminal—George Van Hall was found guilty. When it was proven that the troopers had no search warrants, he was tried again and found guilty a second time. He served his sentence at the

Alfred Seymour was Lansing's chief of police during the Prohibition years and led the department admirably despite the public's disdain for the Volstead Act. *Courtesy of Wikimedia Commons.*

Michigan Reformatory in Ionia. As Lansing police chief Alfred Seymour said, "When the prohibition law went into effect, we didn't bother with search warrants. We just went in and got the liquor." This was probably a good plan, as the evidence could easily be destroyed while the officers made their way through the red tape.

THE COAST GUARD

Established in 1790 as the Revenue Cutter Service, the United States Coast Guard as we know it today was the result of a merger between the Revenue Cutter Service and the United States Lifesaving Service in 1915. It now functions as an arm of Homeland Security. From 1920 to 1933, the coast guard was a major player in the pursuit and arrest of rumrunners. Michigan's Great Lakes area, in general, and the Detroit River, in particular, were in dire need of additional professional law enforcement. Today, Grand Haven is known as Coast Guard City, and each year, it hosts the Coast Guard Festival, the second-largest event in Southwest Michigan. Only Holland's annual Tulip Time celebration attracts larger crowds.

Like other warriors in the fight against smuggling alcoholic beverages into the country, the coast guard was no stranger to controversy. Coast guard personnel were offered incentives to look the other way, and being human, some yielded to temptation. The difference was that a cop caught taking bribes could lose his job, while coast guard sailors who took bribes or stole confiscated liquor were routinely court-martialed. Most served honorably and lived up the service branch's motto, *Semper Paratus*, meaning "Ever Ready" or "Always Ready." By 1923, the coast guard was such an important part of the war on rumrunners that Congress appropriated $13 million to build more vessels and add personnel. The sailors were unpopular among the people around the Great Lakes. Drys thought they weren't doing a good enough job, while the wets resented yet another hurdle to overcome in transporting their liquid assets.

On September 12, 1922, the court docket in Muskegon showed thirty-two cases of liquor law violators. The following year, the city announced it was increasing its enforcement efforts by arresting the wives of hundreds of men who were making homebrew, and it was announced that they would be jailed if it could be proven that they knew about the still. Few if any women were arrested, but the number of stills dropped slightly,

This diagram shows the complexity of smuggling liquor from Canada via the Detroit River and the difficulty of knowing the location of the smugglers. *Courtesy of Wayne State University, Detroit.*

as the risk was too great. With both parents in the slammer, who would take care of the kids? But this didn't discourage the ladies who smuggled. Women were often better than men at getting smaller amounts of alcohol out of Canada, as they weren't searched as rigorously as men. They could wear garments with large pockets under oversized coats, so as long as the contraband didn't rattle or slosh, no one would be the wiser. Some ladies even packed contraband in faux baby bumps. Others transported liquor in watermelons and hollowed-out eggshells, leaving customs officials to wonder why Michiganders preferred Canadian eggs and how they could possibly consume so many of them. The jig was up when one of the egg buyers tripped and dropped her basket.

Who would have suspected nuns of smuggling liquor and conducted a search? No one—that is, until one less than pious "sister" complained, in words not usually used by nuns, of the inconvenience of a flat tire. "She" was caught when the frustration made her slip out of character and speak in a male voice. This was too bad, as the nun's voluminous habits hid a multitude of bottles. Also, pragmatic judges tended to be less forgiving than the kind priests in confessional booths.

6

THE VOLSTEAD ACT TURNED ORDINARY CITIZENS INTO CRIMINALS

Prohibition is better than no liquor at all.
—Will Rogers

The most interesting of the scofflaws were the locals who had, until then, been law-abiding citizens. Then, they went to work producing goods to sell or to serve in newly minted speakeasies, where consumers had to know the password to gain admittance. Every town had enough colorful characters to keep everyone's thirst lubricated.

Two of Kalamazoo's most colorful characters were Harold Curry and Paul Butler, who operated a brewery in the Curry home on Barnard Street. They were arrested when leaving the residence to deliver a truckload of ten-gallon containers. An entrance hidden under the porch revealed a basement containing two thousand gallons of beer and $6,000 worth of equipment and supplies. The partners were rumored to be connected to Al Capone, but no proof was ever found. The river of beer that flowed down Barnard Street when the illegal brew was dumped kept tongues wagging for weeks.

The era inspired an avalanche of cartoons and doggerel. One postcard pictured a man living in a boardinghouse; his liquor supply had been dipped into, and the landlady's cat was falsely accused. The card was mailed in 1924 to Wilbur Van Til of Grand Ledge. The message on the back read, "Do be careful and don't leave your stuff out where the kitties can partake. We all know it's becoming a lot more expensive these days."

The man on this postcard lived in a boardinghouse. When some of his moonshine went missing, the landlady blamed her cat. *Courtesy of the Library of Congress.*

Home production of alcohol was often a family business, as this verse illustrates:

Mother's in the kitchen
washing out the jugs.
Sister's in the pantry
bottling the suds.

Father's in the cellar
mixing up the hops.
Johnny's on the front porch
watching for the cops.
—Anonymous

THANKSGIVING DAY MURDER IN GRAND HAVEN

With the advent of Prohibition, some law-abiding citizens suddenly became law breakers. This may have contributed to a tragedy on Thanksgiving Day in 1922, when Peter Koopman shot and killed his wife, Kate. The couple,

The former Eagle Saloon in Grand Haven is where Peter Koopman killed his wife, Kate. The building is now a shop named Second Impressions. *Photograph by Christine Nyholm.*

who had been married for twenty-six years, had been living a comfortable life with their three children in Grand Haven. Peter owned and operated the Eagle Saloon on Third Street and was a respected businessman. The couple was well regarded in the community. Local newspapers described Peter as a respectable man who "was known to have always conducted an orderly place, had always been a liberal and charitable and a man who inspired friendship." Kate was described as someone who was "well-loved and had many friends in the community," according to Jane Ladley in *Pieces of the Past* on MLive.

Peter may have continued to sell alcohol after Prohibition, which was probably why he was due in court for a liquor violation. After years of prosperity, Peter had built up a comfortable fortune. The income from the saloon went down or was nonexistent due to the constraints of Prohibition. Even after losing his income, Peter continued to spend money lavishly, living beyond his means and spending his savings. The financial stress caused by a lack of income, along with his ingestion of alcohol, may have contributed to his frame of mind.

On that fated Thanksgiving afternoon, the couple was arguing to the point that Kate sent her son to get a policeman. When police went to check on the couple, the building was quiet, so they did not investigate further. That Thanksgiving afternoon, Peter shot Kate in the back. Her body was found the following afternoon at the bottom of the stairs. Their son, Clyde, and Mr. Koopman's attorney, Charles Misner, had to enter the house through a window to search for Peter, who had been due in court that day for a liquor violation charge. No one can say why Peter committed the dastardly crime that ended the life of his wife, but witnesses later reported that he had been drinking heavily that afternoon.

In order to prevent the trauma of making family members and other witnesses testify in court, the prosecution struck a plea bargain with Koopman. He pleaded guilty to manslaughter instead of standing trial for first-degree murder. At sentencing, Judge Cross preached a Prohibition message, stating that Koopman's case was "a lesson to all as to what the moonshine would do. But for the moonshine, he would have been a successful man, his wife would be alive, and his family would have been united and happy." Koopman served a minimum sentence of seven years. There are claims that the ghost of Kate Koopman continues to haunt the building where her life was ended. The former Eagle Saloon still stands as a consignment shop called Second Impressions in Grand Haven.

Woman Hides in Monarch Club Chimney

The Monarch Club was established in Grand Rapids in 1925 and returned with the same name in 2006. The corner business had a drugstore on the first floor and operated a speakeasy on the second floor. According to local legend, there was a police raid at the club one night. One quick-thinking woman dashed into the fireplace and pulled the curtain closed

This hotel room in Grand Rapids shows the result of an unsuccessful attempt at distilling whiskey. *Courtesy of the Grand Rapids Public Library.*

The Monarch Club in Grand Rapids was established in 1925 and operated a speakeasy on the second floor. *Photograph by Christine Nyholm.*

behind herself. She escaped detection but had to endure ridicule as she walked home, crusted in soot and chimney dirt. Today, the Monarch Club operates as a corner bar. It displays a sign behind the bar that reads "Repeal the 18th Amendment."

One trouble with amateur moonshiners is that they didn't always know how. A guest in a Grand Rapids hotel hadn't quite mastered the craft, and his still exploded.

DODGE HEIR ARRESTED IN KALAMAZOO

John Duval Dodge, the eldest son of Dodge Brothers Automotive founder John Francis Dodge, was no stranger to controversy. When he married at the age of twenty-one in 1918, his father was so angry that the automotive pioneer cut his son off and put him on a monthly allowance of $150. This would have been considered a paltry sum, considering that the wealthy

John Duval Dodge appeared in front of Judge Bartlett in a crowded Kalamazoo courtroom to face the charges of drunk driving and a Prohibition violation. *Press photograph from the collection of Christine Nyholm.*

automotive manufacturer was worth an estimated $50 million. John Francis Dodge passed away unexpectedly from influenza in 1920 without providing an inheritance for his eldest in his will. The son contested the will and ended up with a settlement of $1.6 million from the estate in 1921.

When John was arrested in Kalamazoo on March 11, 1922, the story made national headlines. Young Dodge was joyriding with a friend, Rex Earl, when they spotted three young women walking home after a dance. They offered the young college students a ride home, but they were surprised when he sped into the country instead. Recklessly, Dodge wanted to show them how fast his car could go, but his antics terrified the co-eds. One woman, Miss Emmaline Kwakernaak, was so scared that she jumped out of the moving car and was hospitalized with severe injuries. Dodge was put on trial before Judge Bartlett in Kalamazoo. He was accompanied to the trial by his wife, Marie Anne Dodge; his mother-in-law, Mrs. P. O'Connor; and his attorney, John P. O'Hara. Judge Bartlett campaigned against speeders, and the courtroom was packed with people who were curious to see how the prominent citizen would fare in the courtroom. He was charged with driving an automobile while intoxicated and transporting liquor, which was illegal under the Volstead Act. He pleaded not guilty to driving at thirty-two miles per hour, but he did plead guilty to driving while intoxicated, according to the *New York Times* on March 17, 1922.

The trial came to a halt when Mrs. Dodge interrupted the proceedings by suffering a nervous breakdown. She had to be taken to a hospital, which must have added to the chaos in the courtroom. Was it the courtroom drama that caused Mrs. Dodge's breakdown or was it the shocking revelations about her husband's extracurricular activities? Her nervous breakdown seems to have occurred after the prosecution had ended and when the defense witnesses had been called to testify. The two arresting officers, Deputy Sheriff Britt Preston and Patrolman Heywood, testified that Dodge was intoxicated. The two female passengers, Miss Ethel Clemens and Miss Sue Stegenga, testified that, although his pal Rex Earl was drinking in the car, John had not been drinking while driving. It is very possible that both testimonies were true, as he could have been drunk before getting behind the wheel, but that could not be known, as breathalyzers had not been invented yet. Dodge was fined $1,000 on the Prohibition violation of transporting alcohol.

KALAMAZOO

Kalamazoo County got a head start on prohibition, banning the sale of alcohol in 1915. Once Prohibition became the "law of the land" in 1920, the law was nothing new in Kalamazoo, but the town's head start did not make enforcing the law any easier than it was elsewhere. The bars of Kalamazoo's notorious Saloon Row on East Main Street, which is now Michigan Avenue, were closed. Arnold "Dutch" Van Loghnen's saloon on Burdick Street, which featured a monkey that collected payments from patrons, was also closed. Newspaper accounts reported police raids and criminal trials regarding the efforts that were made to prevent bootlegging and the sale of alcohol, according to "Sins of Kalamazoo in Museograph" in the spring 2009 issue of *Kalamazoo Valley Museum.*

To stem the tide of illegal activities, the Kalamazoo Police Department hired Orville Sternbough as a special officer in 1920. Sternbough recorded his activities with the vice squad daily from June 1922 to August 1929. The journal is now in the Western Michigan University Archives. Sternbough described arrests for drunkenness, the suspicion of drunkenness and the possession or sale of alcohol. The officers would sometimes just confiscate the liquor, but other times, they would arrest and book the suspects. Raids on illegal distilleries were common. During a three-month period in 1924, police raided thirteen distilleries; most of them were small operations with 5- or 10-gallon stills. There was one distillery on Fourth Street that had a 20-gallon boiler and 250 gallons of rye mash. Sternbough also reported on a raid that was conducted with the Michigan State Police. They seized equipment, a 50-gallon still and fifty-two 1-gallon barrels of liquor on a Texas Township farm.

Kalamazoo police also worked to close the speakeasies, where patrons could imbibe alcohol and party. In 1923, police raided a bowling alley, cigar store and pool room in a location that is now known as the Corner Bar. One ambitious night in August 1928, police raided six speakeasies. On a different night, they discovered alcohol being served at the Keystone Club, which was above the Rose Tire Company, a location now occupied by the Kalamazoo Valley Museum.

Perhaps the busiest law enforcers were those in the St. Joseph area, as they had to deal with the shenanigans of the locals and Al Capone and his associates. In 1903, St. Joseph officials thought they had permanently fixed their liquor problem by making saloon owners and their bondsmen pass examinations by the new city council reform committee before they could renew their licenses. Six of the eighteen were forced to close, as they failed to meet the new standards of respectability. In just a few years, "St. Joseph" and "respectability" would not be used in the same sentence.

7

ORGANIZED CRIME

I don't even know what street Canada is on.
—Al Capone when asked about selling Canadian liquor

Actually, Al Capone had no reason to know Canada's location, as he was getting his moonshine from Detroit's Purple Gang. He didn't sell it as is, however, as he increased his profits by turning it into "needle whiskey" by injecting water and other liquids into it, thereby making his initial investment stretch further.

Before the Volstead Act was ratified, the manufacture and distribution of alcohol was the fifth-largest industry in the country, and it may have risen higher afterward. We'll never know because if records were kept, they were not shared. One thing was certain: boatloads of money were being made, and not a penny of it produced tax revenue. Al Capone considered that a good thing when he was arrested for tax evasion. "They'll never make it stick," he is reported to have said. "They can't legally collect taxes on illegally earned money." Unfortunately for Al, they not only could, but did. When that happened, Scarface threw himself a lavish going-away party at the Vincent Hotel in Benton Harbor in Berrien County. Ever the optimist when it came to his activities, he rationalized his business by saying, "When I sell liquor, it's bootlegging. When my patrons on Lakeshore Drive serve it on a silver platter, it's hospitality."

It's interesting to note how many of the most violent of career criminals cut their teeth on bootlegging and rumrunning. Scarface wasn't the only professional criminal who was active in Southwest Michigan. George "Dutch" Anderson ended up here, too. He dabbled in petty theft but gave in to the temptation of armed robbery and would eventually turn his attention toward robbing trains and banks. After immigrating to the United States around the turn of the nineteenth century, he briefly attended the University of Wisconsin but dropped out after discovering that crime did indeed pay—and paid handsomely. The only problem was that he hadn't yet fine-tuned the art, and he kept getting caught, thereby becoming acquainted with the inside of various prisons in various states. A burglary conviction earned him a cell in New York's Auburn State Prison, where he met bank robber Gerald Chapman. They formed a partnership after their paroles in 1919. Some states, including Michigan, had already ratified the Volstead Act, so the time was ripe for a new career in bootlegging. They also began operations in Toledo, Miami and New York over the next two years.

In late 1921, along with another Auburn alumnus, Charles Loeber, the two bootleggers began committing armed robbery. The three men forced a U.S. Mail truck to stop at gunpoint, taking $2.4 million worth of cash, bonds and jewelry. They eluded capture for more than eight months and were eventually arrested by New York police on July 3, 1922, after being betrayed by a police informant. Anderson received a twenty-five-year sentence to be served at Atlanta Federal Penitentiary in Georgia. After serving only a year and a half, he escaped from prison on December 30, 1923, and was suspected by authorities to have rejoined Chapman.

GEORGE "BABY FACE" NELSON AND THE GETAWAY CAR THAT GOT AWAY

A young thug named Lester Joseph Gillis began his legendary career in crime as a teenager in Chicago. Later, he worked for Al Capone but was dropped from the payroll when it became obvious that he was trigger-happy and had too short a fuse. It's hard to believe that anyone could be too violent for Al Capone's gang, but Scarface preferred careful planning over spontaneous combustion. Eventually, Gillis took on the name George Nelson. It's uncertain how he acquired the nickname "Baby Face." While most believe it was because of his five-foot-four-inch height and boyish appearance, others have attributed it to a description given by a robbery victim.

In 1931, two armed robberies gave him two one-year-to-life sentences in Joliet Prison in Illinois, but he somehow managed to acquire a gun that he used to escape from custody while still in transit. He then fled to California, where he found employment working as a guard for bootleggers. But like the song says, "Chicago keeps calling me home," and a year later, Nelson answered the call. Back in his hometown, he quickly teamed up with Eddie Bentz for the purpose of robbing banks and decided on the People's Savings Bank in Grand Haven, Michigan. Bentz was the only member of the crew with bank experience, as he had also worked with Machine Gun Kelly. The others participating in the heist were Earle Doyle, Chuck Fisher and Tommy Carroll. Another inexperienced man known only as Freddie was the designated getaway car driver and had been ordered to wait outside in the Buick and be ready to roll.

Nelson's time in Grand Haven, though brief, was comically memorable. A bank located on the corner of Washington Street and Third Avenue was the site of his humiliation. When Nelson pulled a Thompson submachine gun on the teller, the teller pressed his foot on the alarm. Unfortunately for the robbers, the alarm sounded not only in the police station but also in the furniture store next door that was owned by Ed Kinkema. As soon as Kinkema heard the alarm, he grabbed his shotgun and tore outside to play hero. When Kinkema spotted the Buick, poor Freddie found himself in a scenario he had not anticipated. One look at the shotgun and he put the pedal to the metal. Meanwhile, the police had arrived on the scene, and Kinkema was rounding up an armed posse of Grand Haven citizens.

Nelson and the gang heard the ever-growing crowd on the street and grabbed bank employees to use as shields as they ran to the Buick. That's when they discovered the getaway car had gotten away. Both teams began shooting. Nelson spotted a car with a woman driver and her children. The desperadoes held a brief discussion about whether or not they should take the children as insurance but decided against it. With or without hostages, the car proved a bad choice, as it soon spluttered to a stop, out of gas. *Oops*! No problem, they simply stole another one. That one blew a tire.

Amazingly, there was only one injury and no fatalities on that day. A later fatality occurred when either Pretty Boy Floyd or one of his partners ordered a hit on Freddie, the driver of the runaway Buick. The blunder-ridden robbery has since been compared to the Keystone Kops or *The Gang That Couldn't Shoot Straight*. If nothing else, it proved the ruthless man who would claw his way up the criminal ladder until he became public enemy number one wasn't quite ready for the big time. In those days, robbing a bank was not a federal crime, so all the bandits had to do was make it over the state line, as police officers could not chase a known bank robber over a state line. That changed in 1934, with laws stating that anyone robbing a FDIC-insured bank could be chased and apprehended anywhere.

BOOTLEGGING AND THE CARROLL LAW

Most of the liquor that came into the United States during Prohibition was transported from Canada, across the Detroit River and into the Detroit area. Once the alcohol was on U.S. soil, bootleggers had to transport it to the customers. Capone's Chicago was a major market for the illegal trade, so that meant traveling the highways between Detroit and southwestern Michigan. The large rural areas in Michigan also offered hiding places for the booze. Bootleggers might have rented space in farmers' barns to temporarily store the booze.

In order to hide their tracks, bootleggers devised clever shoes to hide their footprints. The shoe, called a cow shoe, had an attached platform that made it look like the footprints had been made by cattle instead of men. This camouflaged their footsteps so that they could escape detection. Much like drug detection dogs of the present day, canines were trained to track people as well as substances. Hooch hounds could detect the smell of liquor and could therefore ferret out hidden bottles in pockets and other hiding places.

A vehicle was the quickest and easiest way to get the liquor to Chicago, where speakeasies and blind pigs were willing customers. Bootleggers with access to the biggest and best vehicles took advantage of the roadways between Detroit and Chicago to deliver their goods.

An incident in Michigan led to a major change in search and seizure laws across the country, making it easier for Prohibition agents and police to catch criminals. Federal prohibition agents Cronenwett, Scully and Thayer and Agent Peterson had been watching bootleggers George Carroll and John Kiro for weeks but had been unable to catch them violating the Volstead Act. One night in December 1921, the bootleggers were spotted on the highway between Detroit and Grand Rapids. They were pulled over sixteen miles east of Grand Rapids. Agents searched the vehicle and found sixty-eight bottles of booze hidden in the backseat upholstery. The agents arrested Carroll for violating the Volstead Act.

Bootleggers strapped on cow shoes to camouflage their tracks when they walked through dirt fields so that they looked like cattle tracks. *Courtesy of the Library of Congress.*

A hooch hound finds a bottle of alcohol in the pocket of a man who is fishing. *Courtesy of the Library of Congress 3b42820u.*

A police dog being trained to detect alcohol. *Courtesy of the Library of Congress 42719a.*

Carroll appealed his conviction all the way to the Supreme Court, claiming it had been an illegal search because the officers didn't have a warrant. The Fourth Amendment of the United States Constitution protects individuals' right to privacy, forbidding unlawful searches of property. However, the Volstead Act provided an exception to the requirement for a warrant, allowing officers to conduct searches of cars, boats and airplanes if officers believed the vehicle was carrying contraband, specifically intoxicating liquors. The Supreme Court ruled that law enforcement officers may conduct a search of a vehicle without a warrant if they have probable cause. The ruling, which allowed law enforcement officials to conduct a search with probable cause, was a major change in law enforcement guidelines for police across the United States.

THE MICHIGAN STATE POLICE

The Michigan state police were established in 1917 to fill the void left when the National Guard was called into active duty during World War I. The advent of automobile transportation made travel across the state and across the country easier and more common for everybody who had access to a car. Trips that previously took days could then be made in hours. This was a great convenience for many honest citizens, but it also was a boon to criminals moving illegal alcohol and other goods across the state. The increased mobility of citizens made it difficult for local police departments to enforce the law. In response to the new challenges to law enforcement, the Michigan State Police Department was formed in 1917.

Bootlegging in Michigan became so widespread that an average of four thousand bootleggers' vehicles were seized every year during Prohibition. The seized vehicles were spruced up and sold at annual auctions, which provided enough funds to pay for 77 percent of the annual budget for the state police.

Michigan State Police troopers pose next to their car. *Courtesy of the Michigan State Police.*

Port Huron troops of the Michigan State Police, who were actively involved in the effort to stop the Detroit River rumrunners. *Courtesy of the Michigan State Police.*

Michigan State Police Corporal Samuel Mapes Killed by Chicago Bootlegger

Michigan State Police corporal Samuel Mapes was just thirty-three when his life was cut short during a traffic stop near Sturgis on May 1, 1927. Corporal Mapes saw two suspicious vehicles on Highway M-23, which is now U.S. 12, a few miles west of Sturgis. The highway was known as a major thoroughfare for transporting alcohol from Detroit and Canada to the thirsty speakeasies and seedy blind pigs of Chicago. A weighted-down Packard, which fit the profile of a "booze runner," was being driven by an African American man. The Packard was following a Wills–St. Claire roadster, a vehicle that was made in Michigan between 1921 and 1926. Suspicious, Mapes pulled the Packard over. The roadster also pulled over, and the Caucasian driver got out of the car and walked back to ask Mapes why he had stopped the Packard. Officer Mapes responded by asking what was in the Packard, to which he received the reply that it was a load of flashlights. A quick search of the Packard revealed that the back of the car was loaded with Canadian hooch.

It was obvious to the bootlegger that he was going to be arrested, so he offered Mapes a hefty $300 bribe to let them go. Mapes could easily have pocketed the money, which was a substantial amount in 1927, but he refused the bribe. He arrested the two drivers but did not handcuff them, which turned out to be a fatal mistake. Mapes flagged down a passing motorist, Mrs. Harold Townsend, who ended up being a witness to the events that followed. Mapes asked Mrs. Townsend to go to Sturgis and summon assistance to bring in the vehicles. His back was turned to the suspects, and while his attention was diverted, the roadster driver was able to grab Mapes's German Luger from his holster, spin the trooper around and shoot him point-blank in the chest. Stunned, Mapes grabbed at his holster and cried, "My God, they've got my gun." He then fell to the ground, unconscious. He subsequently died on the way to the hospital. The bootlegger casually walked to his car and threw the pistol into the backseat. He then motioned for the driver of the Packard to follow him, and they proceeded west. The two cars drove a short distance before the Packard driver stopped his car and told the killer that he was through. The two drivers switched cars, and the killer left the driver on the side of the road with the roadster and took the Packard. He drove the backroads to Chicago to elude capture.

The tragic incident led to an extensive manhunt for the killer. The Michigan State Legislature authorized a $500 reward for the arrest and capture of the murderer. The *Lansing Capital News* editorialized:

> *A reward of $500 is little enough. We would like to see a reward of $2,500 posted anytime a state policeman is killed. Chicago whiskey runners ply the roads in the best and fastest cars that money can buy. They are backed by money and utterly defiant of law enforcement officers. Only recently, word has been put out by Chicago gangsters that they intend to run whiskey through Michigan regardless of the attitude of the state. This is a challenge to the state of Michigan by the most corrupt ring in America. The answer of a sovereign state power of Michigan should come quickly.*

State Police lieutenant Lawrence Lyons and his fellow officers were determined to capture the murderer, who they suspected was a rumrunner. Armed with meager descriptions from Mrs. Townsend and other witnesses, they started their investigation at Ecorse, a major loading point for the trafficking of alcohol between Detroit and Chicago. They were able to identify Chicago bootlegger Charley Coffey as a likely suspect.

Coffey had been arrogant enough to pay for some alcohol shipments with checks, so the police were able to track down his address through a bank in Chicago. They found that Coffey was living under the name Al Johnson with his wife and daughter in the Windy City. Michigan detectives Ray Ferris and Arthur Trease, along with five Chicago policemen, set a trap for Coffey at his residence. Coffey approached his house in the Packard, but something must have alerted him of danger, as he gunned the car past the house, leading the police on a wild chase through the busy city streets. The chase ended when Coffey crashed into a brick wall, and he was apprehended. The police also caught his African American chauffeur, Claude Smith, and another accomplice, Buford Chumm.

The police found Mapes's handgun in Coffey's garage, and the criminal soon confessed to the murder. He later stated to Lieutenant Fred Armstrong that he only intended to kidnap and release the officer, claiming that the gun fired accidentally. Coffey was transported to Kalamazoo County Jail, arraigned before a Sturgis justice and ordered to stand trial at the St. Joseph County Circuit Court in Centerville. Police rallied to gather witnesses to aid in the prosecution in case Coffey recanted his confession. They subpoenaed thirty-eight witnesses, including accomplices Claude

Mapes Hall at the state police administration building in East Lansing was dedicated to fallen Michigan State Police trooper Samuel Mapes. *Courtesy of the Cadillac Wexford Public Library.*

Smith and Buford Chumm. Coffey's daughter, Dorothy, who was with him when the crime was committed, also testified. She was able to verify that Mapes had turned down the $300 bribe. The week-long trial was followed by a jury deliberation of only twenty minutes before Coffey was pronounced guilty of first-degree murder. On July 27, 1927, Judge Clayton T. Johnson pounded his gavel and sentenced the rumrunner to life in the Jackson prison.

The Michigan State Police remembered Colonel Mapes when they dedicated their new headquarters in East Lansing in a ceremony held on March 13, 1929. Speakers at the dedication ceremony included Governor Fred W. Green; Lyon G. Adams, the superintendent of the Pennsylvania State Police; Attorney General Wilber M. Brucker; and Roy C. Vandercook, the first commissioner of Michigan public safety, according to a 1929 article in the *State Journal* of Lansing. Governor Fred Green made a compelling statement during the dedication ceremony, imploring that Coffey never be released from prison. Green said:

> *Corporal Mapes was murdered by a man named Coffey, who has behind him money and influence. As governor, I have felt this influence working for his release. Governors to come in Michigan will feel this influence. I have one request I would like to make to my successor. I would like to ask him never to pardon the man who killed Mapes and pass on to his successor the same request. I would like to have Michigan's line of governors to never pardon the murderer of a police officer and have that sentence of life imprisonment prove to be just what it was intended to be, a life sentence.*

Mapes Hall cost $90,000 to build and was equipped with the modern amenities of the era. The stalwart building served as an administrative office on the Michigan State Police complex for several decades but was demolished after the police headquarters was relocated to another building in 2010. Colonel Mapes continues to be recognized as a pioneer in criminal patrol and investigation through the Colonel Samuel A. Mapes Award, which was created in 2016. The annual award is presented to Michigan state troopers who are proactive in "looking past the traffic stop" to excel in proactive criminal patrol and investigations.

MUSKEGON DETECTIVE CHARLES HAMMOND IN DEADLY SHOOTOUT WITH GANGSTER DUTCH ANDERSON

The city of Muskegon drew national headlines in the aftermath of a fatal shootout between Detective Charles Hammond and notorious gangster Dutch Anderson. Detective Hammond was a forty-eight-year-old family man. He and his wife, Clarissa, had four children, Clifford, Douglas, Nathan and Ferol. He was described as a giant of a man at about six feet two inches tall and about 235 pounds. He was well liked and respected by his fellow police officers.

Dutch Anderson was one of the most wanted criminals in the United States. His partner in crime, Gerald Chapman, had been recaptured on January 18, 1925, in Muncie, Indiana. Anderson and Chapman had spent time at the Muncie farm of Ben Hance, who had a record of small-time bootlegging. Anderson blamed the farmer for informing on Chapman and retaliated by gunning down Hance and his wife. The couple paid the ultimate price for getting involved with dangerous criminals. His picture was on posters across the country, but he escaped detection by changing his appearance, moving around and keeping a low profile. Anderson was traveling around Michigan and keeping under the radar to elude capture. He made cash by passing off counterfeit money, a relatively low-level crime for a criminal of his stature. It was in Muskegon that a merchant became suspicious of a twenty-dollar bill.

It was around 7:00 p.m. on Halloween night, October 31, 1925, when a dapper-looking Dutch Anderson went into the Colonial Tea Shop on Western Avenue. He purchased a box of candy for $1.25 and was going to pay in exact change but gave Mrs. Ingalls, the manager and wife of the owner, a $20.00 bill instead. She completed the transaction but became suspicious and sent her son, Garcia, across the street to the Muskegon Savings Bank to verify whether the bill was legitimate. The bank clerk declared that the bill was counterfeit, and Garcia went to the police headquarters to report the matter. Charles Hammond, the detective on duty, asked Garcia Ingalls to accompany him to look for the man who passed the counterfeit bill.

Events may have unfolded differently if Hammond's partner, Detective William Feeney, had been there, but as fate would have it, he was late that Halloween night. Hammond and Feeney had worked together on many criminal investigations, including the daring daylight payroll robbery at Lakey Foundry just three months earlier. Hammond was working alone at

The Muskegon Savings Bank, where it was learned that Dutch Anderson's money was counterfeit, is now the 18th Amendment Spirits Co. *Courtesy of the Hackley Public Library in Muskegon.*

the beginning of the shift and likely felt he could handle the matter of a counterfeit bill on his own. Of course, he did not know that he would come face to face with one of the most dangerous wanted men in the country.

The detective asked Ingalls to walk with him to see if they could spot the man. They only walked about a half block before they spotted him in Sanford Drugstore. Hammond waited outside for Anderson, and after he left the store, he told him they needed to talk at the police station. Anderson was polite and compliant and did not seem to present a problem, so Ingalls departed and left Hammond to handle the matter. As the men walked together, they were among people with lanterns and children dressed in costume for Halloween. At one point, a little girl stopped in front of them and blew a horn in their faces. They grinned and she skipped away. At the corner of Jefferson, Hammond turned his prisoner around and started toward the police station. They walked a half block and started across the alley toward the fire station.

Anderson took Hammond by surprise when he suddenly wrenched away and sprang free to dart up the alley. Hammond pursued the prisoner, still not knowing his identity. The criminal whipped out his pistol and shot back at Hammond. Anderson grabbed a woman named Mrs. Alex Campbell and momentarily used her as a shield as he opened fire at the detective. Terrified pedestrians scattered to escape the gunfire. Bullets passed through the windows of the fruit stand and Joe Matel's Cigar Store on the opposite side of Jefferson Street. Hammond caught up with Anderson in the alley and was shot several times. It is not known why he never drew his own gun, but it is possible that he was not able to access his weapon in the pocket of his new overcoat or that he was worried about the danger of gunfire around the hostage and the citizens on the street. In spite of suffering several gunshot wounds, Hammond was able to catch up with the criminal and wrestle the gun from his hand. He shot Anderson at close range with the criminal's own gun. Both men were mortally wounded and collapsed at the rear of the city hall building.

George Thompson, another police officer, arrived at the scene and was able to shoot Anderson as he tried to get up. Later, ballistic tests found that the fatal bullet was fired by Hammond with Anderson's own gun. Even though he was wounded, Hammond, with the help of a fellow officer, was able to stagger into the police station and tried to salute to Chief Hansen.

The Muskegon Police Department in front of the statue of President McKinley in Muskegon. *Courtesy of the Hackley Public Library in Muskegon.*

His last words were: "Here is his gun, but he got me." He was rushed to Hackley Hospital but died two hours later, never knowing he had put an end to the criminal career of a notorious gangster. The identity of the criminal was the subject of excitement and speculation. At the time of his death, Anderson had over two thousand twenty-dollar counterfeit bills on his person. Impressions of his fingerprints were inked, and the FBI identified the man as George "Dutch" Anderson.

Tributes to Charles Hammond poured in from around the country. The posted reward money for the capture of Dutch Anderson was turned over to the Hammond family. In addition, *Liberty Magazine* contributed $1,000 to the family of the fallen officer. The *Muskegon Chronicle* organized a fund drive to help the family. Flags were flown at half-mast, and thousands of people paid their respects at Balbirnie Funeral Home and at the Central Methodist Church, where services were held. The City of Muskegon erected a handsome marker at Hammond's grave site at Oakwood Cemetery.

Dutch Anderson remained a mysterious figure even after his death. Several days after his death, attorney William J. Baker from Rochester, New York, published an article in Rochester newspapers. Baker had represented Anderson in the past and was a confidant of the criminal. The article stated that Anderson's real name was Ivan Dahl Von Teller and that he had been born in Denmark to a wealthy Danish family. He frequently wrote to his mother, who believed that her son was a successful American businessman. The criminal was unceremoniously buried in the same cemetery as Hammond. The stone, which was paid for by Baker, was a simple marker that identified him as George Anderson—followed by a question mark.

Realizing that Dutch Anderson had been in Muskegon, the secret service investigated further and believed that he had been in Bitely with his gang from Toledo during the Lakey payroll robbery a few months earlier. The robbers had conducted a daring daylight robbery of Lakey Foundry and got away with a bonanza of nearly $33,000. Bitely is located in Newaygo County and is a short drive from Muskegon. The secret service concluded that Anderson and his gang had committed numerous crimes throughout Michigan during the months preceding his death. Five months after Anderson's death, his criminal partner Gerald Chapman was executed for killing a police officer.

The Charles D. Hammond Fraternal Order of Police (FOP) Lodge #99 in Muskegon is named in honor of the courageous detective. In 2000, the FOP Lodge #99 donated a memorial statue in honor of Hammond and other Muskegon police officers who had lost their lives in the line of duty.

The Protectors memorial, which pays tribute to Muskegon-area police officers who died in the line of duty, was donated by the Charles D. Hammond Fraternal Order of Police Lodge #99. *Photograph by Christine Nyholm.*

The memorial, named *The Protectors*, now lists the names of thirteen officers who died between 1908 and 2017. The statue is installed in front of the hall of justice in Muskegon.

AL CAPONE MAKES SOUTHWESTERN MICHIGAN A VACATION PLAYGROUND

The western coast of Michigan was a popular vacation area for people looking for a getaway in the early twentieth century. The beautiful coastal area offered sandy beaches on the shores of Lake Michigan as well as entertainment, music, amusement parks, theater and more. Freshwater springs were reputed to have healing qualities, which attracted the health-conscious to soak in and drink the waters. The area was also attractive to a criminal element, who enjoyed the many amenities of the region. It probably didn't hurt that it was a convenient stopping point for bootleggers transporting liquor from Detroit to Chicago.

Southwestern Michigan was a vacation playground for Al Capone and many of his gang members. The lakeside cities of Benton Harbor and St.

Above: Health-conscious people enjoy the waters at the Silver Queen of Eastman Springs in Benton Harbor instead of drinking alcohol. *Photograph from the collection of Christine Nyholm.*

Left: Al Capone, the most notorious gangster of the Prohibition era, vacationed in Berrien County. *Photograph, circa 1930, public domain.*

Joseph were just two-hour drives from Chicago, so it was easy to drive from the big city to the lakeside resort area. The region became a retreat and meeting place for the who's who of the underworld. In addition to the gangsters who stayed at the hotels in the area, some of Capone's men purchased houses in the region. Capone's bodyguard Phillip D'Andrea had a large house, or mansion, in St. Joseph. Another bodyguard, Louis Campagna, purchased an eighty-acre farm in Berrien Springs, which was later owned by boxing great Muhammad Ali. Other gang members who had properties in the area included Jake Guzik, Edward Konvalinka and Paul "The Waiter" Ricca DeLucia.

Capone, along with members of his notorious gang, was known to stay at the Whitcomb Sulphur Springs Hotel in St. Joseph and the Vincent Hotel in Benton Harbor. The criminals patronized several local establishments, where they became popular for passing out big tips to the hotel bellhops, restaurant servers and other workers. The people in the area knew they were Chicago gangsters but treated them royally anyway because they anticipated big tips and the needed boon to the economy. The gangsters were careful to be polite and respectful and were not seen as troublemakers. Although they seemed to be friendly, they did carry the tools of their trade, deadly handguns and machine guns, as sometimes witnessed by locals. Capone's favorite spots in the area also included the Berrien Hills Country Club, the "Little Italy" District and the

The Whitcomb Sulphur Springs Hotel in St. Joseph was one of the hotels patronized by Al Capone and his gang members. *Photograph postcard from the collection of Christine Nyholm.*

The Whitcomb Sulphur Springs Hotel and Lake View Hotel on Lake Michigan attracted guests and bootleggers from Detroit and Chicago. *Photograph postcard from the collection of Christine Nyholm.*

House of David Amusement Park. Everywhere they went, they generously passed out five-dollar bills as tips, which endeared them to townspeople.

The young caddies at Twin City Golf and Aviation Club would line up for the privilege of working for Capone because he tipped generously and would buy them an ice cream cone. Capone was a mediocre golfer, but he apparently enjoyed the game and was eager to improve. Capone and his men would also have spa treatments and massages at the Hotel Saltzman and Mineral Springs in Benton Harbor. The Vincent Hotel Beauty Shop would close for the day when Capone's gang would come in for grooming treatments. The men would get haircuts, manicures and eyebrow jobs, while their wives, or molls, were pampered with beautifying treatments, such as haircuts and styles, according to the book *A Killing in Al Capone's Playground* by Chriss Lyon.

The Israelite House of David was a religious commune located in Benton Harbor. The group had strict rules, so members were not allowed to drink alcohol or smoke. They followed a strict vegetarian diet and were discouraged from having sex. The men were not allowed to cut their hair, so many of them had beards and long hair that cascaded to their waists. While the Christian group had strict rules, it did know how to have fun and

The House of David Israelite Band from Benton Harbor performing in New York City. *Courtesy of the Library of Congress 3b22367.*

entertain visitors. The group's amusement park was complete with a band shell and popular miniature train. It had a brass band that performed to the delight of the crowds. Perhaps the most famous of all was its nationally acclaimed semi-professional baseball team. Capone reportedly went to a practice baseball game at the House of David and wanted to see the men with long hair—or as he referred to them, "the men who looked like girls." The gangster was frustrated to see that the men's long, luscious locks were tucked under their caps. Despite Capone's demands, the men refused to remove their caps or reveal their hair.

While Capone tried to keep a friendly profile with the people of the area, some of his men were hard to control. Reportedly, some of Capone's gang members frequented the Twin Gables Hotel and Restaurant, now the Hotel Saugatuck, in Saugatuck. The hotel website states that, according to local legend, there is a bullet hole in the wall of the Sandpiper, which was the hotel's bar. One of Capone's men had a sweetheart working in the kitchen, and it is possible that another man made a pass at her. The gang member allegedly made his feelings known by shooting the hole in the wall.

Pretty nurses and a dog pose in front of the John Robinson Hospital in Allegan, where Al Capone's gang members were reportedly taken for medical treatment. *Photograph from the collection of Christine Nyholm.*

The John Robinson Hospital in Allegan was also reputed to be a refuge for Al Capone and his men. The Greek Revival building was built in 1909 and purchased by a doctor from Chicago in 1920. When Capone's men needed medical care, such as that required for bullet wounds, they would get treated at this hospital.

VALENTINE'S DAY MASSACRE IN CHICAGO TOUCHES BERRIEN COUNTY

Capone was the most famous and feared of the gangsters of the era, and he continues to be known as the face of bootlegging and violence during the Prohibition era. The bloody Valentine's Day Massacre in Chicago was tied to Berrien County through one of Capone's men, a gangster named Fred Burke. The massacre was an act of violence between rival gangs on February 14, 1929. Capone and Bugs Moran were rivals vying for control of the bootlegging trade and other criminal enterprises. Men posing as police officers entered the S.M.C. Cartage Company garage at 2122 North Clark Street in Chicago, where several of Moran's men were hanging out. It is believed that the victims thought the intruders were, in fact, police officers there to arrest them, so they put their hands up and turned toward the wall. They were shot down and killed in a hail of bullets fired from Thompson machine guns. Ironically, Moran himself was not with his men at the time, so he was not killed.

It has long been believed that Capone arranged the bloody shooting of Bugs Moran's crew in the Chicago garage. Capone himself had an airtight alibi because he was in Florida at the time, but it was believed that the massacre took place on his orders. Chicago's top gangster, who was also known as Scarface, was dubbed "Public Enemy Number One." Fred "Killer" Burke was one of Capone's men who operated with a gang that Scarface called his "American Boys." Burke, a suspect in the Valentine's Day Massacre, settled in Berrien County under the alias Fred Dane.

Burke was born Thomas A. Camp in Kansas to a farm family. As a young adult, he embarked on a life of crime in Kansas City, Missouri. He moved to St. Louis, Missouri, and became a member of Egan's Rats, the top gang in the area, before joining the U.S. Army and serving in the military during World War I. He later moved to Michigan and became associated with the Purple Gang in Detroit. The dangerous and notorious Purple Gang controlled the flow of about 75 percent of the illegal liquor into the United States during Prohibition. As part of the Purple Gang, Fred Burke, associate Gus Winkler and some other Egan's Rats associates were suspects in the violent Milaflores Massacre in 1927. A few months after the Milaflores Massacre, Burke and his associates parted ways with the Purple Gang and relocated to Chicago. Al Capone welcomed them into his gang, calling them his "American Boys." They were given special assignments and were involved in murders and armed robberies across state lines, including New York, New Jersey, Kentucky and Ohio.

Following the Valentine's Day Massacre, Burke resided in a rented bungalow in St. Joseph, Michigan, where he was known as Fred Dane. He told people he was an oilman, which is what gas station owners were called at the time. He spent money freely and extravagantly invested $5,000 into turning the rented bungalow into a home that suited his desires. He may have continued to blend into the community if it weren't for a drunken binge that turned into tragedy when he killed a young police officer named Charles Skelly.

Charles Skelly was the son of Gustav and Mary Schultz Skalay, immigrants of German origin who lived in the village of Volhynia, Russia, before immigrating to the United States in 1901. Charles, also called Chuck, was the second child of the hardworking couple, who eventually had eight children.

Left: Fred "Killer" Burke, who killed St. Joseph police officer Charles Skelly, was captured in Missouri. *Courtesy of Chriss Lyon, the author of* A Killing in Al Capone's Playground.

Right: St. Joseph police officer Charles Skelly was a strapping young man who was shot down in his prime. *Photograph from the Heritage Museum and Cultural Center in St. Joseph, provided by Chriss Lyon, the author of* A Killing in Al Capone's Playground.

Tragically, Gustav's wife, Mary Skalay, died in on November 21, 1919, while delivering their ninth child, who only survived a few hours. The Skalay family was large and loving, and they had their share of hardships as they made their way in their new country. Gustav's brother, sister and mother also emigrated from Russia and settled in Benton Harbor, so they had extended family in the region. As an adult, Charles Americanized his last name by changing it to Skelly. He was described as a strapping young man who must have been strong and had a lot of vitality. He worked as the assistant to the chief of the fire department before proudly joining the police force. Like many bachelors of his age, his mind also would have been occupied with the courtship of his pretty girlfriend, a local woman named Mildred Thar.

Ten months after the Valentine's Day Massacre, on December 14, 1929, Charles Skelly was on foot patrol in the town of St. Joseph. The downtown area was festively decorated for the holiday season, and the young officer was seen exchanging pleasantries with people he encountered. As he patrolled, Forrest L. Kool approached him to report that he had been in an accident with a drunken man driving a Hudson Coupe on Highway 12. The Hudson coupe had hit his Chevy and damaged the fender, but the man refused to settle. The drunken man was carrying a roll of $100 bills but said he didn't have enough small change to pay Kool the demanded $25 for repairs. If he had handed Kool one of those $100 bills, the matter might have been settled then and there. Instead, the inebriated man decided to flee the scene.

As Kool was reporting the accident to Skelly, they spotted the Hudson driving by, and the officer recognized him as the new guy in town. He jumped onto the running board and ordered the driver to drive to the police station. Burke must have been terrified that if he went to the police station his identity would have been discovered and he would have been sent to prison for his crimes. He drove a few blocks with Officer Skelly on his running board before stopping at a traffic light. Seeing an opening, Burke lunged for a Colt 45 gun that was stashed in the car's side pocket and shot Skelly three times. Skelly stumbled back in pain and reached for his gun, but the Hudson roared off, leaving the young officer in the street. Bystanders rushed him to St. Joseph's Sanitarium, but the damage was too extensive, and he lost too much blood. He died at 11:10 p.m. that night. Skelly's last words were: "Get that guy."

Making his getaway, Burke roared away but lost control of his Hudson on a sharp curve on Lake Boulevard and smashed up his car. He jumped out and ran through backyards until he found a man named Monroe Wulff, a member of the Israelite House of David. Wulff was sitting in his car and waiting for his wife, but Burke intruded on his plans. Burke jumped into the car and pointed his pistol at Wulff and told him to "beat it south and be quick," according to the Berrien County Sheriff Department's website. In the meantime, Berrien County sheriff's deputy John Lay found the wrecked Hudson. Inside the coupe, he found papers identifying the owner as Fred Dane who lived on Lake Shore Drive. Police now had the name of the suspect—or at least his alias—and knew where he lived.

When Wulff reached Jericho Road, Burke got out of the car and Wulff quickly roared off. Burke then got a ride from an acquaintance named Albert Wishart. Even though Wishart gave him a ride willingly, Burke pulled a gun on him and forced him to drive out of town. He wanted to go to the drugstore and forced Wishart to stop, but when he got out of the car, his ride once again left him on his own. He started walking toward his house, but when he neared the bungalow, he saw that the police had beat him there. An officer named Deputy Kubath noted the shadowy figure approaching the house, but when he turned his lights on, the figure disappeared into the woods. Burke knew the police were hot on his trail, so he ran to a neighbor who was unaware of the commotion surrounding the shooting.

Steve Kunay gave Burke a ride and started driving toward Coloma, but he soon realized that something was very wrong. He said he needed to get gas and left Burke in a park outside of Coloma. When he returned to Stevensville, he saw the police officers at the bungalow. In the search of Fred Dane's residence, police officers soon realized that their suspect was a serious criminal. They found an arsenal of sawed-off shotguns, hand grenades, ammunition, revolvers, tear gas bombs and two Thompson submachine guns. They also found about $390,000 worth of bonds that had been stolen from a bank in Jefferson, Wisconsin, in November, just weeks earlier. A fingerprint lifted from a household object in the house revealed that the suspect was Fred "Killer" Burke, a lead suspect in the Valentine's Day Massacre.

Two Thompson machine guns that were used in Chicago's Valentine's Day Massacre are in the custody of the Berrien County Sheriff's Department. *Courtesy of Chriss Lyon, the author of* A Killing in Al Capone's Playground.

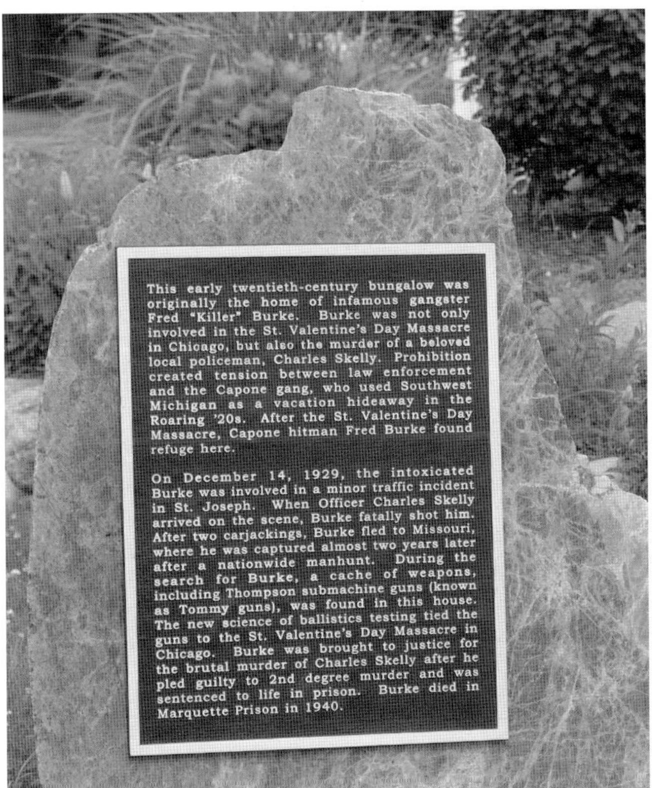

Above: The Benton Harbor bungalow that Fred "Killer" Burke rented, where the Thompson machine guns from the Valentine's Day Massacre were found by police. *Photograph by Christine Nyholm.*

Left: A memorial in front of the bungalow that was rented by Fred "Killer" Burke describes his connection to Chicago crime and the killing of local policeman Charles Skelly. *Photograph by Christine Nyholm.*

Fred "Killer" Burke was on the run, and it was well over a year before he was caught. He managed to catch up with his old pal Gus Winkler and pull off robberies in Los Angeles. The two gangsters knew they were both wanted men, so they went to a plastic surgeon in Chicago and had their appearances changed. Burke had his nose changed from concave to convex and his straight lip was scarred to look like a harelip. Burke was using the alias Richard White when he stayed at a farm owned by Barney Lee Porter in St. Joseph, Missouri. He first presented himself as a farmhand but later took on the persona of a successful businessman. He married the Porters' daughter, Bonnie, who would later claim no knowledge of her husband's criminal history; she said that she just thought he traveled a lot for his business.

He was found in Green City, Missouri, on March 26, 1931, thanks to an astute local gas station attendant who had seen his picture in a *True Detective* magazine. Joseph Hunsaker had been motivated to turn Burke in for the reward money, but by the time the case was processed, the rewards had expired. He was bitter when he only received $250 instead of the originally offered bonanza of over $100,000. Once Burke was captured, there was a question over which jurisdiction would get to take custody of the criminal. In addition to Michigan, he was wanted in Illinois, Indiana, Minnesota, North Dakota, South Dakota, Rhode Island and Wisconsin. Authorities determined that Berrien County had the best case against "the most dangerous man alive," so he was transported to Michigan to stand trial.

Berrien County Circuit Court judge Charles E. White found that Burke was inebriated when he killed Officer Skelly and was therefore unable to form the intent to kill. The charges were dropped from first-degree murder to second-degree murder due to witness testimony that Burke was drunk when he committed the dastardly crime. On April 27, 1931, Burke pleaded guilty to second-degree murder and was sentenced to a life of hard labor at the Marquette State Penitentiary. He died on July 10, 1940, after suffering a massive heart attack.

The arsenal found in Burke's bungalow, including the Thompson machine guns involved in the Valentine's Day Massacre, remains in the possession of the Berrien County Sheriff's Department. The bungalow that Fred Burke lived in has been painted white and is now a Coldwell Banker Real Estate office. A memorial to Officer Skelly was installed on the property in 2019. A detailed account of this case and the people and events surrounding it can be found in the extensively researched book *A Killing in Capone's Playground* written by Chriss Lyons.

8

THE END OF AN ERA

Making Prohibition work is like making water run uphill; it's against nature.
—Milton Friedman

The "Noble Experiment," as it had come to be called, went down in defeat in 1933 with the ratification of the Twenty-First Amendment, which repealed it. As in earlier attempts, a lack of enforcement was a key reason for Prohibition's failure. Also, the supposed social benefits of a dry country, including less drunkenness, more people working and less domestic violence, never fully materialized. The Twenty-First Amendment has been the only amendment ever passed to repeal a previous one.

Money talks, and in this case, it was screaming, so taxation played a major role. None of the money that paid for all of that booze went into Uncle Sam's coffers. Add to this the growing unemployment of the Great Depression and it became obvious that legalizing the liquor industry would put men to work. The money that went into the pockets of the Purple Gang, Al Capone and others like them gave honest working men the cash they needed to feed their families. It wasn't just the organized criminal element that led to the downfall; the law had turned into a game for a formerly law-abiding populace who now delighted in dreaming up ways of outsmarting the enforcers. Will Rogers said it best: "Instead of giving money to fund colleges and promote learning, why don't they pass a constitutional amendment prohibiting anybody from learning anything? If it works as well as prohibition did, why, in five years, we would have the smartest race on earth."

The Wickersham Commission

In 1929, President Herbert Hoover appointed the National Commission of Law Observance and Enforcement to conduct a detailed study on law enforcement in general, but with Prohibition as its primary focus. It was also called the Wickersham Commission, as former district attorney George W. Wickersham served as its chairperson. The group worked for two years before releasing its fourteen-volume report in 1931. The commission's findings confirmed everything that was already known about the difficulties of enforcing the Volstead Act not only in big cities but all across the land. The commission found that more people were drinking after than before Prohibition; there was more criminal activity; criminals included law enforcement officers; the amendment had corrupted both the judicial and political systems; organized crime family members had grown wealthy while the rest of the country was in a depression; and tainted alcohol had become a major health problem. That was the big picture. The commission's members also disclosed isolated incidents that were too numerous to name, like the incident of a widowed mother of young children whose neighbors bought her a still and set her up in business.

When Hoover made the report public, he stated the commission "did not favor the repeal of the Eighteenth Amendment as a method of cure for the inherent abuses of the liquor traffic." He continued, "I am in accord with this view." This stated the obvious: the commission had drawn the conclusion the president wanted.

The eleven members of the commission were themselves at odds. Some favored a compromise law, while others felt the situation could be rectified with stricter enforcement. None dared to recommend repeal, even though they stated (correctly) that Prohibition was impossible to enforce, tax revenues were lost and the majority of the public not only didn't support it but held it in contempt. The entire "Wickersham Report" remains a classic example of not letting the facts influence a decision. When the commission's members stopped scratching their heads in disbelief, both wets and drys claimed victory. The wets could boast that a federally funded major study had verified that Prohibition wasn't working. For their part, the drys claimed the report backed up their claims about the evils of drink. Franklin P. Adams of the *New York World* nailed it when wrote this scathing summary of the commission members and their work:

Prohibition is an awful flop.
We like it.
It can't stop what it's meant to stop.
We like it.
It's left a trail of graft and slime,
It's filled our land with vice and crime,
It don't prohibit worth a dime,
Nevertheless, we're for it.

The repeal of Prohibition was inevitable, as the general public realized the law was an exercise in futility. It had unintentionally released the evils of career criminals like Al Capone and the Purple Gang. It also became impossible to overlook the growing epidemic of deaths attributed to alcohol poisonings. In 1927, the United States alone reported nearly twelve thousand deaths of individuals who had consumed bootleg liquor contaminated with wood alcohol, strychnine, iodine and phenol, to name a few of the poisonous substances found in some of the products turned out by illegal home distillers.

On April 27, 1933, after Franklin D. Roosevelt (a "wet") was sworn in as president, nineteen states were permitted to sell beer; however, the sale of beer was not legalized in Kalamazoo until May 11, 1933. By this time, beer was the only alcohol-containing libation that was allowed to be sold in thirty states. In celebration of the end to Prohibition, Michigan governor William A. Comstock signed a law that allowed people between the ages of eighteen and twenty years old to drink beer and wine but excluded the allowance of hard liquors. Even then, some proponents of Prohibition continued fighting to keep it going. Kalamazoo "dry" groups, including the Allied Citizens for Prohibition, drew up a petition and soon had more than two thousand signatures for the continuation of the Eighteenth Amendment. Not surprisingly, the attempt never gathered the momentum needed to carry it forward. The prolific poet Anonymous made it clear who lost the most with the repeal of Prohibition:

To Prohibition's Ashes:

When Uncle Sam said, "We'll go dry,"
Crooks ceased to mourn the days gone by
And tossed their hats into the sky,
When Uncle Sam said, "We'll go dry."

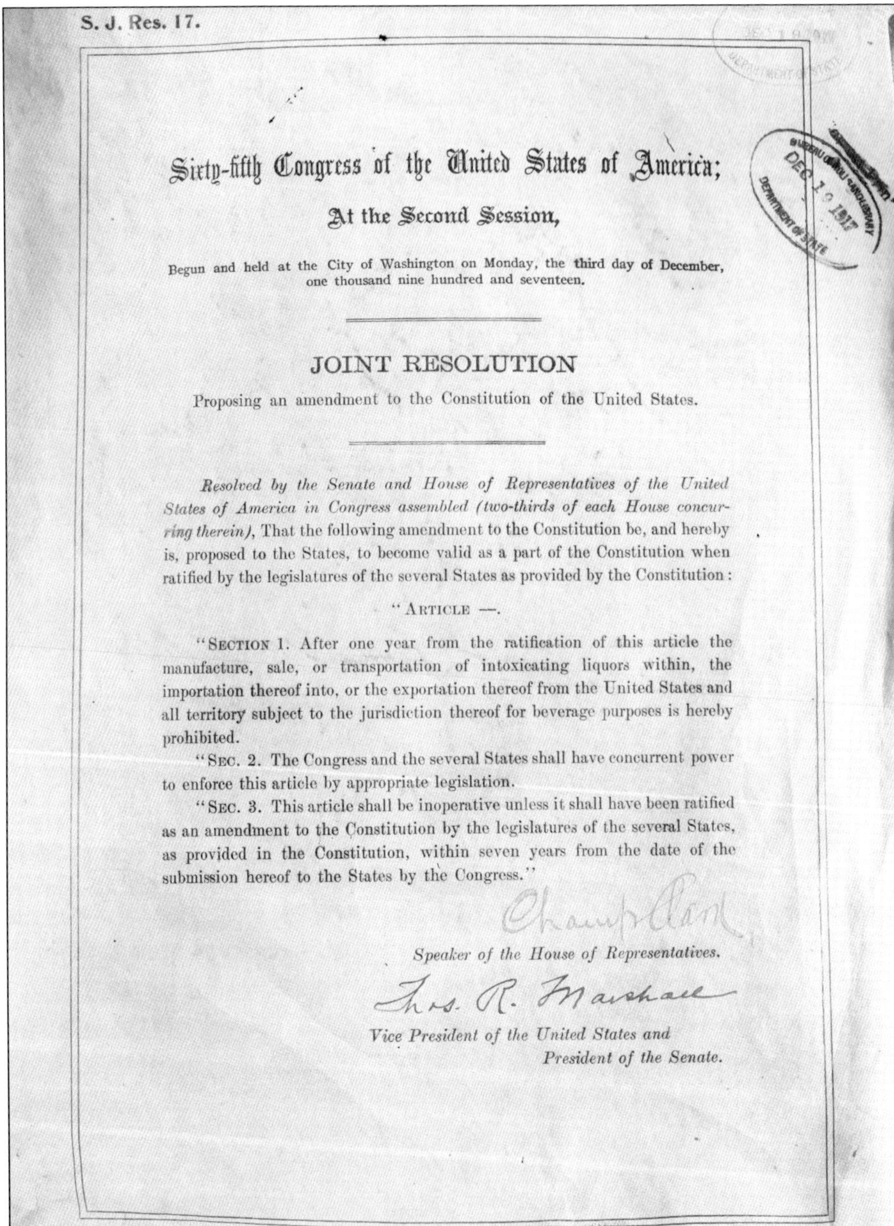

S. J. Res. 17.

Sixty-fifth Congress of the United States of America;

At the Second Session,

Begun and held at the City of Washington on Monday, the third day of December, one thousand nine hundred and seventeen.

JOINT RESOLUTION

Proposing an amendment to the Constitution of the United States.

Resolved by the Senate and House of Representatives of the United States of America in Congress assembled (two-thirds of each House concurring therein), That the following amendment to the Constitution be, and hereby is, proposed to the States, to become valid as a part of the Constitution when ratified by the legislatures of the several States as provided by the Constitution:

"ARTICLE —.

"SECTION 1. After one year from the ratification of this article the manufacture, sale, or transportation of intoxicating liquors within, the importation thereof into, or the exportation thereof from the United States and all territory subject to the jurisdiction thereof for beverage purposes is hereby prohibited.

"SEC. 2. The Congress and the several States shall have concurrent power to enforce this article by appropriate legislation.

"SEC. 3. This article shall be inoperative unless it shall have been ratified as an amendment to the Constitution by the legislatures of the several States, as provided in the Constitution, within seven years from the date of the submission hereof to the States by the Congress."

Champ Clark

Speaker of the House of Representatives.

Thos. R. Marshall

Vice President of the United States and President of the Senate.

A copy of the Eighteenth Amendment of the Constitution. *Photograph by Harris and Ewing, courtesy of the Library of Congress 14201a.*

From every source, the liquor poured
As law went splashing overboard
The conscience sank, the drink-bill soared
And what could not be drunk was stored.

Then Uncle Sam said, "We'll go wet!"
The crooks turned pale and begged, "Not yet!"
Their goose was cooked; their sun had set,
When Uncle Sam said, "We'll go wet."

GONE BUT NOT FORGOTTEN

Today, the Prohibition era is remembered less for its gore and more for the glamour and fun times of the Roaring Twenties.

The area's first winery was St. Julian's Winery founded by Mariano Meconi. The Meconi Wine Company winery had its start in Ontario, Canada, in 1921. When Prohibition was repealed, Mariano took the opportunity to relocate the winery to Detroit and renamed it the Italian Wine Company. When Prohibition ended, the manufacture and sale of alcohol was once again legal, and ambitious brewers and vintners were eager to fill the void left by the rigors of temperance and the Volstead Act. Many of the pre-Prohibition breweries had gone out of business completely and did not reopen. Meconi discovered that he loved the grapes from the Paw Paw area, and in 1936, he relocated his winery to Paw Paw and renamed it St. Julian's Winery. The winery in Paw Paw remains in the center of Michigan's grape-growing region, the Lake Michigan Shore Appellation, and it still uses local fruit in its vintages. The family-owned winery is the most awarded winery in Michigan and now offers wine and spirits in six locations.

The second-oldest winery in Michigan, Warner Vineyards, was founded in 1938 and is located right next to St. Julian Winery. Warner Vineyards was founded by John Turner and James K. Warner as an adjunct to the family farming, banking and farm supply businesses. The winery is situated on the riverbank in Paw Paw. They have restored the old waterworks building and have a historic 1914 Grand Trunk railcar in front of the building.

St. Julian's Winery and Warner Vineyards, in the heart of Michigan's wine country, are central attractions at the well-attended Paw Paw Wine and

The WCTU fountain in Spring Lake was donated by the Woman's Christian Temperance Union in 1910 to encourage drinking water instead of alcohol. *Photograph by Norma Lewis.*

Harvest Festival, which is held annually. The festival celebrates the bounty of the region and includes several community events. Visitors are welcome for tours and tastings year-round, so Paw Paw is a wine-drinkers' destination even when the festival is not in session. The Paw Paw wineries are just two of the popular establishments that celebrate the "fruit of the grape" in Southwestern Michigan. Wine aficionados and people who just want to learn about wine and taste various vintages can find several unique wine-drinking experiences in the region. The number of wineries in the region shows that there is a demand for the pleasurable beverage.

Craft beers are trendy, and Southwestern Michigan has embraced the trend. Instead of having to operate in secret, brewers boast of their various craft ales and beers. The oldest and largest craft brewery in Michigan is Bell's Brewery, which was founded in 1985 in Kalamazoo. Prior to Prohibition, Grand Rapids claimed to have the most breweries in Southwestern Michigan.

Left: Louie's Trophy House in Kalamazoo may have been a speakeasy during Prohibition. *Photograph by Christine Nyholm.*

Below: The Cottage Bar in Grand Rapids got its liquor license in 1933, and it is still a popular bar and restaurant today. *Photograph by Christine Nyholm.*

Today, the city has returned to its love of brewing beer, proudly claiming the moniker "Beer City USA." There are a host of popular craft breweries, including Atwater Brewing Co., Grand Rapids Brewing Co., Brewery Vivant, the Mitten Brewing Co., Perrin Brewing, Harmony Brewing Co. and many more. There is no shortage of locally made brews to experience in Southwestern Michigan.

In addition to locally made wines and hand-crafted beers, there are locally made meads, hard ciders and distilled beverages to be found. Mead is also called honey wine and is made from honey produced by bees. The oldest alcoholic beverage in the world, mead has had an artisanal renaissance. Hard ciders, a popular beverage with early immigrants, are available at local cideries. The distilleries offer a view of how hard alcoholic beverages are produced and give customers a chance to taste locally made liquors, such as whiskey, brandy, vodka and gin. It is a far cry from the secret backrooms, back passageways and basements that often housed the speakeasies of the Prohibition era.

In recent years, it has become trendy to drink in establishments resembling the old speakeasies. Like the original speakeasies, the establishments range from dive bars to elegant drinking and dining establishments. While the ambiance might be similar, the major difference is that patrons do not have to worry about being arrested just for being present. Today's watering holes offer the ambience of a speakeasy without requiring a password to gain admittance.

Some pubs that may or may not have been speakeasies are still going strong, including Nick Fink's in Comstock Park, Monarch Club in Grand Rapids, Schulberg's in Big Rapids, Louie's in Kalamazoo and Win Schulers in Marshall. The Cottage Bar in Grand Rapids opened during Prohibition but never sold alcoholic drinks until after the Twenty-First Amendment was ratified. The owner holds one of the first liquor licenses issued in the city. The Eighteenth Amendment Spirits Company serves food and drink at the former Muskegon Bank, which played a key role in the shooting of Muskegon police detective Charles Hammond by Dutch Anderson. It features an ambiance true to the era and offers membership to its popular Scofflaw Society. Members receive discounts on menu items and merchandise, an etched Eighteenth Amendment glass, a subscription to Scofflaw Society emails, admittance to members-only events and other benefits. In a nod to the style of speakeasies, Al Capone's Speakeasy in Muskegon is not identified by a sign; instead, the frosted window in the door reads "Anti-Saloon League, Chicago Branch, Est. 1920." The distinguished Amway Grand Hotel in Grand Rapids has opened IDC, an acronym for "I Don't Care," a 1970s-style speakeasy on the second floor of the historic Pantlind wing. Patrons must obtain a passcode, which changes monthly, to enter the speakeasy.

Cheers!

SELECTED BIBLIOGRAPHY

Fox, Craig. *Everyday Klansfolks: White Protestant Life and the Ku Klux Klan in the 1920s*. Lansing: Michigan State University, 2011.

Lyons, Chriss. *A Killing in Al Capone's Playground*. Holland, MI: In-Depth Editions LLC, 2014.

Massie, Larry. "Massie's Michigan." *Encore Magazine*, February 2011.

Pardoe, Blaine, and Victoria Hester. *The Original Battle Creek Crime King*. Charleston, SC: The History Press, 2016.

Smith, Leanne. "Peek Through Time: Bootleggers, Bank Robbers Who Passed Through Jackson Foiled by Michigan State Police Officer Edd Freeman." MLive. www.mlive.com.

INDEX

L

M

N

O

P

R

S

T

V

W

ABOUT THE AUTHORS

Norma Lewis has lived in Southwest Michigan for about thirty years in total and is now living in Grand Haven. She loves local history and enjoys the thrill of the hunt when doing research, mainly because she almost always finds something better than what she thought she was looking for. This is her seventeenth book and her ninth with Arcadia Publishing and The History Press. Along with local histories, she writes for children, including picture books about animals who engage in goofiness.

Christine Nyholm has always lived in the Great Lakes region, where she made a career in business sales and marketing in Milwaukee and Chicago. She currently calls beautiful Grand Haven, Michigan, home. She has a variety of interests and has written online about a variety of topics, including entertainment, travel, history, health and more. This is her third book about local topics in Michigan, with her other titles including *Images of America: Muskegon* and *100 Things to Do in Grand Rapids Before You Die*.